Edition 7

INSIDER'S GUIDE
TO THE
WORLD OF PHARMACEUTICAL SALES

Principle Publications

Jane Williams

ISBN: 0-9704153-6-2
Seventh Edition
Editor: Lorraine Griffin
Cover Design: Lorraine Griffin

Library of Congress Control Number: 2003112390

Published and Printed in the United States of America

Previous Editions

ISBN: 0-9704153-5-4 Sixth Edition, Published April 2002, Out of Print
ISBN: 0-9704153-4-6 Fifth Edition, Published June 2001, Out of Print
ISBN: 0-9704153-3-8 Revised Fourth Edition, Published 2000, Out of Print
ISBN: 0-9704153-2-X Fourth Edition, Published 2000, Out of Print
ISBN: 0-9704153-0-3 Third Edition, Published 1999, Out of Print

Questions may be directed to:

Principle Publications
4101 W. Green Oaks Blvd. • Suite 305-585
Arlington, TX 76016
principlepublications.com

Reviews

Professional Review:

"My goal and role as a professional resume writer is to market my clients in such a way that their resume will lead to a job interview. After getting the interview, however, their ultimate goal is to get the job. Finding and recommending the ***Insider's Guide to the World of Pharmaceutical Sales*** is the best thing I have ever done for my clients to aid them in the process of being successful in their quest of a career in pharmaceutical sales.

"This is the definitive information and "how-to" book in this field, and after reading the book, a seasoned salesman with many years of sales experience told me, 'I had the best interview I have ever had. Every question was right out of the section of questions very recently asked by pharmaceutical sales companies.' A social worker desirous of getting into this field said, 'I now have the confidence that I can do this job.'

"If you are seriously interested in a career in pharmaceutical sales, you <u>must</u> read this book and arm yourself with the knowledge of this industry that will make your interview an outstanding one and that will set you apart from other interviewees."

Lois Jobe, C.P.R.W.
Certified Professional Resume Writer
ASAP Resume Services
Web site: DynamicSalesResumes.com

Professional Review:

"Jane Williams has supplied her readers with a powerhouse of information in an easy to read, concise format. The *Insider's Guide...*is an absolute necessity for anyone seriously considering a career in pharmaceutical sales."

Lorraine Griffin
Editor, Resume Authors

Professional Review:

"Jane Williams' fabulous book, 'Insider's Guide to the World of Pharmaceutical Sales' (6th edition) is a MUST-READ for any resume writer who works with individuals wanting to get into pharmaceutical sales — and it's a book you can recommend to your clients as well."

Bridget Weide, C.P.R.W.
Editor, Resume Writers' Digest

Customer Reviews:

"I know it's been a while since I last contacted you. I've been working extremely hard to get into the business. I followed your book to the letter and last week I received a job offer from ___Pharmaceutical! The salary, bonus, and perks are way more than I ever imagined I could get!

"I prepared my "brag book" just like you recommended. It definitely helped the interviewer get to know me. The way I found out about this job opening was from the local rep, so I had the inside track the whole way. The hiring manager just happens to believe in hiring people that do not have pharmaceutical experience yet so they can be trained.

"I think I got lucky to get a biotech job, but I was extremely prepared and ready for the interviews. I went out for "ride-alongs" and made a comparison between my last job and the pharmaceutical salesman duties.

"Thank you for your book! Someone recently told me that they were interested in getting into pharmaceutical sales. I told them the first thing they should do is to get your book! Thanks again."

Dave J.
New York, NY

"Just wanted to let you know I studied your book cover to cover and did everything you said to do and after three (very smooth) interviews I won a pharmaceutical sales position! Thanks."

Mary C.
Orlando, FL

_____

"Thank You VERY much for your assistance and promptly answering my questions. I honestly did not expect you to get back to me this quick. I have followed your book thus far and would highly recommend it to anyone trying to get their foot in the door as a pharmaceutical sales rep. The only regret I have is not ordering your book 6 months ago. I could not have come this far without your insight. Keep up the excellent work!"

Regards,

Kam R.
San Diego, CA

_____

"Jane, you are terrific!

"Four weeks after purchasing your guide, I've got the job!!! The district manager kept asking me HOW could I possibly know so much about the job if I hadn't worked as a rep. It was great!"

John S.
Omaha, NE

"I wanted to thank you for the excellent information I found in your book. I did exactly as you suggested and landed a pharmaceutical sales job the first try within a division of (major pharmaceutical company). I was told that I could put a feather in my hat for impressing everyone that I met. I was even offered more than I asked for."

Andy G.
Phoenix, AZ

_____

Dear Jane,

"I wanted to email you sooner but I have been extremely busy studying for my NEW JOB as a sales rep!!! Thanks for all of your help through your great book and excellent advice! I appreciate all of it as I am sure others do too! It is great knowing there are still people who are willing to help others succeed and I will always remember that. I now have a great job with a good company selling top of the line drugs."

Thank you, Nancy J
Chicago, IL

"Thanks for such a great guide. I recently purchased your Insider's guide and read it cover to cover. I then read through all of the sample questions and applied to several companies. I received calls for interviews within 2 days and now two weeks later I already landed a job with a Major Pharmaceutical company. They indicated the reason I was given the job over other candidates was because of the "Sales Presentation" I made comparing their major antihypertensive product with another competing product. I feel that if your customers take the time to review the guide and practice their answers they will all be as lucky as I was."

Matthew P.
Columbus, OH

_____

"Well, I had my interview with (major pharmaceutical company) this morning and it went very well! They were impressed with my personal binder and all of the information that I had gathered about their company. I've been invited back for the second interview!

"Thank you again. I don't think I could have prepared so well without your guidance. I've never felt so prepared for an interview as I do for this one - and that is due to your guide and your wonderful advice!"

Pam T.
Atlanta, GA

*See our web site at http://www.principlepublications.com for a complete listing of success stories.

Table of Contents

Preface

CHAPTER 1: PHARMACEUTICAL INDUSTRY FORECAST gives an overview of the pharmaceutical sales industry and details why I am certain that this industry is recession proof!

CHAPTER 2: ANY DEGREE IS THE RIGHT ONE explains why any four-year degree is acceptable for a pharmaceutical sales career. This chapter also lists the preferred degrees for entry-level pharmaceutical sales positions and for promotion to trainer and district manager.

CHAPTER 3: PHARMACEUTICAL SALES REPRESENTATIVE describes everything from a typical day in the life of a pharmaceutical sales representative to the detailed profile of duties performed by a veteran pharmaceutical sales representative.

CHAPTER 4: NETWORKING explains how to keep someone from "closing the door" in your face! This chapter teaches you how to contact sales representatives, the "keys" to entering the pharmaceutical sales industry, how to set up "Field Preceptorships" and how to get to the person with the "power to hire."

CHAPTER 5: RESUMES AND COVER LETTERS outlines the different types of resumes and gives examples of each. Included in this chapter are details describing how to craft a pharmaceutical sales industry-specific resume with the correct format and "keywords" to prevent you from making mistakes that will exclude you from the interview lists! This chapter also gives complete instructions on creating a great cover letter and includes examples.

CHAPTER 6: ONE OF THE CHOSEN FEW teaches you how to make the most of the professional contacts that you have made...how to network successfully. Professional appearance and creating a winning plan of action are also stressed.

CHAPTER 7: SELECTING THE RIGHT COMPANY teaches you how to research and evaluate companies for their employment stability and your personal ability to "match" with the company.

CHAPTER 8: PHARMACEUTICAL COMPANY REQUIREMENTS is a great chapter because you will learn exactly what type of candidate the pharmaceutical sales industry is seeking to fill its positions. You will find insightful information about the pharmaceutical sales company "mindset" and what it looks for in personality and selling style for new hires. I believe in creating your own luck and tell you how to do this by "setting yourself up for success!"

CHAPTER 9: INTERVIEW PREPARATION is an extremely important chapter! This chapter explains what you must know about the interviewing company, products, management style and different types of interviews. Additionally, you are taught to prepare a "personal presentation binder" that includes a career-comparison document, with example, to help you sell yourself, especially if you do not have sales experience.

CHAPTER 10: INTERVIEW QUESTIONS AND ANSWERS is the single most important chapter! This chapter contains 150 of the most recent pharmaceutical sales interview questions with correct answers! Included are questions such as:

    a. What is "co-promotion" or "team-selling?"
    b. How do you see a "no see" physician?
    c. "SELL ME SOMETHING!" directive. How do you sell the interviewing district manager something, especially one of his/her company's products?

The answer consists of a detailed pharmaceutical sales interview answer with examples that have won positions for my customers worldwide!

CHAPTER 11: THE RIGHT STUFF! Here you will find questions you should ask yourself to see if you have what it takes to really be successful as a pharmaceutical sales representative.

CHAPTER 12: PURPOSE AND RESPONSIBILITY explains what a pharmaceutical sales representative's responsibilities are.

CHAPTER 13: CAREER PATH AND PERKS supplies information that everyone loves! This chapter explains the various positions available within the industry in addition to the different types of compensation and benefits.

CHAPTER 14: CONTRACT SALES ORGANIZATIONS offers a listing of the major contract sales organizations complete with addresses, phone and fax numbers and web site addresses.

CONCLUSION

APPENDIX A: PHARMACEUTICAL COMPANY PROFILES offers 28 top pharmaceutical company profiles. Information included on each company consists of: company address and contact information; company background information including mergers; annual revenue, research and development; sales force size and total number of employees; major products with therapeutic area and pipeline products.

APPENDIX B: PHARMACEUTICAL COMPANIES lists 300 pharmaceutical companies and their web site addresses so that you can easily find any major to moderate sized company, along with many smaller companies that you may need to research.

Author

Jane Williams is a former award-winning pharmaceutical sales representative, a professional pharmaceutical sales consultant, and a recognized authority in the pharmaceutical sales industry who has been interviewed several times by the Dallas Morning News. She sold medical equipment and laboratory services for Roche Biomedical, one of the biotechnology giants, and won sales awards in this position before gaining a position with another major pharmaceutical company. During her nine years in pharmaceutical sales, Ms. Williams was promoted to a position as a pharmaceutical sales field trainer because of her ability to sell and to teach others how to sell and quickly became certified in that capacity. While still serving as a certified pharmaceutical field sales trainer, Ms. Williams was promoted into a specialty sales representative position where she excelled and is a multi-time winner of the highly coveted President's Club Award presented to the top sales leaders in the industry.

Due to numerous pleas for help from people who wished to gain positions as pharmaceutical sales representatives, Ms. Williams decided to write a guide to help anyone who wanted to become a pharmaceutical sales representative. Because of her years of experience and the knowledge she gained from hundreds of pharmaceutical sales representatives that she has known through the years, she has accomplished the task of writing a complete guide to gaining a pharmaceutical sales position. The *Insider's Guide to the World of Pharmaceutical Sales* presents everything you need to know to gain a pharmaceutical sales position in a neat, easy to read, outline format.

Ms. Williams left the pharmaceutical sales industry to become the National Sales Director for Principle Publications. There she maintains contact with pharmaceutical sales representatives, specialty sales representatives and sales managers. This allows her to stay in close touch with the pharmaceutical industry to ensure that every edition of the *Insider's Guide to the World of Pharmaceutical Sales* contains the most current and relevant information available to assist those people who aspire to join one of the most prestigious career fields in the sales industry, pharmaceutical sales.

Introduction

Introduction

Why is the pharmaceutical sales industry one of the mostly highly sought after sales career fields available today? Personal growth and, very often, uncapped income potential make this career extremely popular. Working as a pharmaceutical sales representative is almost like having your own business without having a downside. A pharmaceutical sales representative organizes, prioritizes and makes independent decisions about his or her business (territory) on a daily basis. The pharmaceutical sales representative doesn't have to worry about start-up capital, losses and employees. Every dollar earned is pure profit!

With starting salaries plus bonuses in the $50,000 range, pharmaceutical sales jobs are some of the highest paying jobs in the job market. When one adds the many benefits, including a company car and insurance, retirement, 401k, education reimbursement, and health insurance, this position is immediately worth over $70,000 per year. That is just the beginning! What other industry offers this type of compensation to new college graduates with a B.S. or B.A. degree? Virtually none! For those who have work experience, the pharmaceutical sales industry still offers more money and greater opportunities than most industries. Many job seekers have made successful career transitions into the pharmaceutical sales industry. You will find people with every type of work history imaginable employed within the pharmaceutical sales industry. That is one of the unique characteristics of this career. Diversity in all areas is valued and recognized as key to the continued success of the pharmaceutical sales industry.

The opportunities for personal and professional growth within the pharmaceutical industry are outstanding! This is an industry where it is possible to move up into management and to retire. That makes the pharmaceutical industry one of the most highly prized industries today with which to secure employment. The competition is fierce! Getting into the business requires more effort than many "jobs" but this is a lucrative career, and it is well worth the effort.

The ***Insider's Guide to the World of Pharmaceutical Sales*** is filled with practical information based on the knowledge and experience of hundreds of ***pharmaceutical sales representatives*** and colleagues from every major pharmaceutical company in the world, who have shared their success stories and their challenges with me over the years.

Gaining a pharmaceutical sales position is what this guide is all about! By securing the ***Insider's Guide*** you have taken one of the most important steps you will ever take during a lifetime of work experience. The information you learn in the ***Insider's Guide*** will fully prepare you for that series of interviews which you must pass in order to enter the pharmaceutical sales industry. As you read the ***Insider's Guide***, you will discover not only how to secure a position within the pharmaceutical sales industry, but you will become acquainted with the mind-set of the industry and the expectations you must meet after you gain the pharmaceutical sales representative position. In addition, you will acquire the information necessary to become an "award-winning" pharmaceutical sales representative so that you may excel in your new position. While no one can guarantee your success or employment in the pharmaceutical industry, you can stack the odds in your favor if you follow the recommendations in this guide so…Let's get started!

Pharmaceutical Industry Forecast

How Secure Is Your Job?

Everyone worries about job security. While there are no guarantees, the pharmaceutical industry is one of the most secure, stable industries today. Why do I believe that it is secure? People will always suffer from illnesses and they will always need treatment with prescription drugs. As our population ages, more lifesaving drugs will be needed. The life expectancy now is approximately eighty years. We know that the older we become, the more likely we are to suffer illnesses that require pharmacological treatment. This job isn't a fad or a technological craze; the pharmaceutical industry is a necessary one.

According to the Pharmaceutical Research and Manufacturers of America (PhRMA), pharmaceutical industry sales in 2002 were an estimated $197 billion. This represents a 10% increase in revenues. U.S. pharmaceutical companies alone invested more than $32 billion dollars in research and development in the year 2002. United States pharmaceutical companies invest a larger percentage of their sales income in research and development than any other industry. More than three billion prescriptions were filled in the United States in the year 2000 according to the "Prescription Drugs: Continued Rapid Growth," September 2000 issue. Pharmaceutical and biotech companies received FDA approval for 89 new drugs including 17 new molecular entities (NMEs) and 9 new biologics in 2002. Additionally, 172 previously approved medications received new indications. New indications require clinical trials and FDA approval as do new drug applications. These new pharmacology products and biologics will treat diseases such as AIDS, arthritis, cancer, glaucoma, cardiovascular disease, infectious disease, anti-inflammatory disease, respiratory and neurological disease.

PhRMA President, Alan F. Holmer, stated in a press release January 25, 2002 that a study conducted by Dr. Frank Lichtenberg of Columbia University shows that replacing older drugs with newer drugs increases prescription costs by $18 each but reduces overall healthcare costs by $111. Prescriptions tend to be the most cost-effective and generally noninvasive form of treatment.

What's in the pipeline? A PhRMA survey reveals the following pharmacological entities and treatment areas:

- 402 new medications for the treatment of various types of cancer
- 123 new medications for the treatment of cardiovascular disease
- 83 new medications and vaccines for the treatment of HIV/AIDS
- 176 new medications for the treatment of neurological disease

This is the result of research and development efforts of more than 100 pharmaceutical and biotechnology companies.

The growth within the pharmaceutical sales industry continues at an impressive rate year after year. With the reauthorization of PDUFA, Prescription Drug User Fee Act, in 2002, new drug applications can be processed in less than eighteen months. This allows the United States to approve new drugs as fast here as they are approved in European countries as well as the rest of the world. Now approximately half of all new drugs approved are approved first in the United States. Recent IMS Health data shows that more than 70% of the total number of prescriptions being taken are the result of the population taking more prescriptions. Even so pharmaceutical spending represents only 10% of the total health care dollars spent.

Additionally, PhRMA Code on Interactions with Health Care Professionals was voluntarily adopted in April 2002. This code governs the pharmaceutical industry's marketing practice, specifically the industry's marketing to physicians and other health care personnel. The new PhRMA Code became effective July 1, 2002. Because this code supports good medical practice and maximizing patient benefits while allowing the best products to achieve sales success, a win-win situation is created for all parties.

What Is Down-sizing or Right-sizing?

We've all heard about down-sizing. Employers down-size when there are more employees than are necessary to get the job done. They also down-size as a means of survival when profits aren't good. "Right-sizing" is basically the same as down-sizing. It just sounds better. The goal is the same. Get the most you can get out of what you have, and maximize your profit. Pharmaceutical companies have done this at times and this could always happen again. Fortunately, most pharmaceutical companies appear to be having excellent growth with new products being launched almost every week.

What if the worst should happen and they down-size? They just won't hire new people for a little while. They will then get new products and expand their sales forces again. **The key to survival is to do your job well.** You're not likely to suffer during a down-sizing if you are a valuable employee. Those who don't perform as well will suffer during down-sizing.

Will the Industry Grow?

Absolutely! As I mentioned earlier, you must have a market for products. Our population is aging and the market is growing. The elderly make up the largest group of prescription takers. As our population continues to age, the need for pharmaceutical drugs will only increase. Of course, this doesn't mean that all people of all ages won't need medicines because they will. Money will continue to pour into the research and development of new drugs because this is necessary for our survival and improved quality of life. The increased lifespan of our population has been attributed in part to the increase in production and the availability of new medications. The impact of an increased lifespan has created a net income increase of approximately $2.4 trillion or greater than 20% of our gross domestic product according to the PhRMA 2003 profile report.

Pharmaceutical and biotechnology companies continue to be strong performers overall in the stock market. Obviously, the pharmaceutical sales representative will to be needed as long as people inhabit the earth. I am sure you will agree the future is a very bright one for the pharmaceutical sales representative.

Any Degree
is the Right One!

Any Degree!

Why is any degree right? Until very recently there were no degree programs available offering pharmaceutical sales degrees, so companies make judgments on an individual basis. Some universities have just started offering a Bachelor of Science in Pharmaceutical Science: Marketing and Management Track. A few colleges/universities offering degrees or curriculum appropriate for prospective pharmaceutical sales careers are: The University of Mississippi, Western Michigan University and The College of St. Catherine. Because the degree is so new, those interested in pursuing this degree should contact universities they wish to attend to see if they offer this course of study. Of course a degree in this area does not guarantee employment. Keep this fact in mind when considering your area of study.

Any person with a B.S. or B.A. and an acceptable Grade Point Average is a potential candidate for a pharmaceutical sales position. Of course, a 3.0 G.P.A. or higher will be viewed in a more positive light than a lower G.P.A. An accredited university/college must grant the degree, and the individual university's scholastic ranking will be taken into consideration by most interviewers. Why will pharmaceutical companies hire English majors over Biology/Pharmacy majors at times? A science background is great, but the name of this game is SALES! One can have all the knowledge in the world about pharmacology and not be able to sell. The pharmaceutical representative must be an intelligent individual, who possesses the right type of personality, in order to succeed in a very competitive industry. *That leaves the field wide open to all college graduates with four year degrees and above!*

Preferred Degree

Biology is usually the preferred degree for an entry-level sales position. Pharmaceutical representatives must be able to learn pharmacology. The new representative must also be able to understand anatomy and physiology as it relates to pharmacology and disease states. Pharmaceutical companies know that if a person has succeeded in gaining a degree in this field, they already have the right foundation for learning pharmacology. They also have solid foundation knowledge of anatomy and physiology. These people will be easy to teach. They can learn the "science" involved in pharmaceutical sales. That is only part of the equation, though; the right personality is at least equally important, if not more important.

Science over liberal arts. While biology is the preferred degree, any science degree provides good background knowledge for pharmaceutical sales. Once again, companies will see the graduate with a science degree as good potential pharmaceutical representative material because the person has mastered the science course work. Solid science knowledge is a major advantage to the pharmaceutical representative; however, the bright student who has the desire to learn can master this information.

Why Is A Degree Necessary?

Company interpretation. How does a pharmaceutical company interpret your degree? What does it mean to a potential employer? The fact that you have had the tenacity to go to school for four to five years, earn a high G.P.A., and complete what you have started, tells the company much about you. The pharmaceutical company knows that you are determined. You have staying power. You don't give up easily. When the going got tough, you got tougher! You didn't quit! Pharmaceutical companies know that the learning skills and personality traits which helped you achieve a college degree are the same ones which will help you gain success in the world of pharmaceutical sales. They know that, basically, you have the "right stuff." The potential to turn you into a "first-class" sales representative is a real possibility. You have the most important basic requirement for a pharmaceutical sales career when you have a bachelors degree from an accredited college/university. Without this, you would automatically be screened out, and denied the opportunity to even interview for a position in pharmaceutical sales.

Advanced Degree

Do you have an advanced degree? If you do, you have an edge over those with bachelor's degrees. Pharmaceutical companies prefer sales representatives with masters degrees. Once again, this is a good indication that you are capable of learning everything and anything that you need to know in order to sell the company's products. Since pharmaceutical representatives call on physicians, they are constantly in contact with some of the brightest minds in our society. In order to carry on intelligent conversations and have mutual understanding, representatives must also be bright and educated. Those who have persevered through six or more years of school, also make an important statement. The completion of the advanced degree offers proof of their ability to learn complicated material, organize, and use wise time management. They obviously have the personality traits of persistence and commitment that it takes to succeed in the pharmaceutical industry.

Advanced degree advantage. *Business/Marketing is the preferred advanced degree*. Those with advanced degrees and good sales records are more likely to be promoted to management positions than those individuals with a bachelor's degree. Companies encourage their employees to gain an advanced degree and most reimburse approved education expenses. This is a wonderful way to pursue a master's degree while you earn a great salary, and get your cost of education reduced significantly! A company gains educational clout with increasing numbers of advanced degreed employees. In the world of business, this elevates their ranking because increased levels of education are generally associated with increased business success.

Why would this be the preferred advanced degree for careers in pharmaceutical sales? After gaining a promotion to district manager or higher, one would need more management skills in addition to the sales skills. At this level, the ability to manage, not just a group of sales representatives, but also a budget and a marketing plan, becomes a necessity. This is where business skills and the art of negotiation become even more critical. Advanced business degrees prove extremely useful to those who have acquired them.

Pharmaceutical Sales Representative

What do pharmaceutical sales representatives do?

Pharmaceutical sales representatives market products to physicians, pharmacists, and hospitals. Pharmaceutical sales representatives market a pharmaceutical company's products using materials and methods approved by that company.

How are pharmaceutical sales representatives trained?

After a sales representative is hired, the representative will be placed immediately in some type of training program. That training program normal consists of all of the following:

- **Home Study**. Usually, the new hire is given anatomy, physiology and pharmacology study materials along with sales materials. The new hire studies for one to two weeks before being tested on the materials. If the new hire makes an acceptable score the new hire is scheduled for the initial training class. If the new hire does not make an acceptable score, a sales trainer will work with the new hire to get that person up to speed on the materials.

- **Initial Training.** Initial training class is where the real work begins. This class is extremely difficult! There is an excellent chance that you will work harder than you ever have in any class that you've ever attended. Why? You will not only have to master the anatomy, physiology and pharmacology study materials, and take more tests, but you will have to pass product sales presentations and demonstrate all of the new selling skills that you have learned. Your sales presentations will be taped, reviewed and critiqued. Your strengths and weaknesses will be discovered. Is this stressful? Of course, it is. Is it worth it? You bet it is! The sales trainers will help you become the best pharmaceutical sales representative that you can be and the **best** earn the most.

- **Sales Meetings.** Sales meetings at all levels usually incorporate sales training classes into the schedule. For example, during district meetings you will present products to your teammates. They will do the same and then everyone discusses these presentations and learns from their team members. New product information is introduced as well as new goals. It's a great learning experience and a very pleasant one.

- **Sales Workshops.** All of the pharmaceutical companies offer mandatory sales workshops for their pharmaceutical sales or territory sales representatives. The purpose of offering the workshops is to keep the sales force in top shape by constantly improving their selling skills.

- **Advanced Sales Classes. Pharmaceutical** sales representatives who show initiative or proficiency in their profession are often encouraged by their company to achieve even better results so the company offers advanced sales classes for them to attend. The advanced sales classes cover a specific selling environment such as the hospital, specialty area, government or managed care selling environments. These classes are designed to further enhance the selling skills of those pharmaceutical sales representatives who have been selected for promotions into advanced sales positions.

A Pharmaceutical sales representative's typical day:

Pharmaceutical sales representatives meet with physicians through preset appointments and through "cold" calls, unscheduled meetings with physicians. During these calls, the sales representative will present information on a company specific product following the guidelines established and approved by the pharmaceutical sales employer. On an average day a pharmaceutical sales representative will:

- Present their product to 8-10 "office-based" and/or "hospital-based" physicians.
- Average two (2) pharmacy calls (sales presentations to pharmacists) per day.
- Average one (1) hospital call (sales presentations to physicians, key medical personnel, and pharmacists) per day in some territories.

What is a product presentation?

Product presentations are the primary sales responsibility in a pharmaceutical sales representative's job description. During a product presentation a pharmaceutical representative will:

- Open a product discussion by making an attention-getting statement or asking a question.
- Describe or paint word pictures of patient types and disease states so that the physician will identify with the presentation message.
- Explain how your medication will benefit the patient AND the physician.
- Supply an indication, mechanism of action, contraindications, side effects and dosing information on the product.
- Overcome objections or simply supply additional information through the use of proof sources such as medical studies and visual aids.
- Present cost-effectiveness and therapeutic advantage information. This is important and a concept that has proven very effective over the past several years as compared to just covering efficacy and side effects as was emphasized in the past.
- Ask for the business and gain a commitment from the physician to write prescriptions and/or start patients on the product with samples supplied by you.
- Follow-up on all sales calls with another sales call with the goal of advancing the sale every time.

What is a proof source and how is it used?

Proof sources are written documents that prove claims you have made. Proof sources commonly used by pharmaceutical sales representatives are:

- pharmaceutical company "visuals"
- pharmaceutical product studies
- "sales aids"

Maintain product knowledge.

The sales representatives are responsible for knowing and staying current on their company's products and information, as well as knowing and staying current, on the competitor's products and information. This goal is accomplished by: company meetings, classes, mailings, literature, e-mails and voice mail messages. These are all part of an educational package provided by the pharmaceutical company to keep the sales representative's product knowledge and competitive knowledge current.

Organize territory.

There are different methods used to organize territories based upon the company's plan of action. Some of these methods are:

- **Call Planner.** This varies from company to company, but basically it is a list of the physicians in the representative's territory. The company will rank the physicians based on the pharmaceutical company's knowledge of the physicians' specialty, the physicians' prescribing habits, and the physicians' potential to write prescriptions for your product. This helps the representative to know where time would be best spent.

- **Territory Analysis**. Companies may provide most of the information for a territory analysis. The representative may also be required to access information for this analysis. This analysis will cover geography and different medical institutions, as well as different physicians in a specific area.
- **Future Projects And Products**. Based on company information, decisions about calling on different institutions, physicians and pharmacists, etc. will be based on what is in the "pipeline." **The "pipeline" refers to research projects and developmental pharmaceutical products.**

Prioritize Activity.

Where should the representative work? What should the call frequency be?

The territory location, district manager, and representative's knowledge will determine where one should spend most of one's time. Basically, the representative uses the company resources available to determine where the business is in the territory. The pharmaceutical company will determine the targeted physician's potential to write prescriptions for the company's products. This information helps create the sales representative's call planner. In other words, this information tells the new pharmaceutical sales representative which physicians should be called upon.

Call frequency is determined by the territory analysis. Your district manager will be very helpful in providing the necessary information for this decision. All pharmaceutical companies have a sales plan of action and sales goals that help determine where a pharmaceutical sales representative will work. This information also determines how often the pharmaceutical sales representative will call upon targeted customers. How often physicians are called upon is determined by their potential, their actual writing habits and accessibility.

Which projects should gain priority?

Based on the current plan of action and future forecasts, you will be able to decide along with your district manager which projects should be completed first.

Continuing Education.

All major pharmaceutical companies offer assistance to their employees in regard to continuing education. Most have in house on-going CE (continuing education) programs that are product and company specific. These are necessary to keep the representatives up to date on their products and to sharpen those very necessary selling skills.

When sales representatives are hired by pharmaceutical companies, they are all given pharmacology and anatomy information to study and learn. They are also given specific product and disease state information to study and learn. Each company has an "initial training" session where the new hires are evaluated, tested and coached on how to sell. During the course of the sales representatives tenure with the company, the sales representatives will have ample opportunity to attend advanced, continuing education classes through their employer to keep sales knowledge and selling skills up to date.

Most companies also encourage and support the employees desire to further their formal education. Many will offer reimbursement of fees paid in the pursuit of an acceptable advanced degree from an accredited college/university.

Medical Research.

There are different ways to achieve this goal. They are:

- **Company provided literature; aids**. Meetings will be held at regular intervals and these are called **POAs or "plan of action"** meetings. New sales literature including visual aids, studies, article reprints and various selling aides are introduced at these meetings.

- **Internet-medical literature search**. In addition to company provided literature and aids, one may also surf the net for medical literature. ***This literature must always be for your information only!*** Companies have strict policies about the use of literature. No literature may be used on the job without your company's approval. There are valid legal reasons for this. Always follow your company's policy!

- **Medical Library**. This is one of the oldest methods of acquiring medical information. Any major hospital will have a reasonably sized library and relevant information can be obtained there.

- **Medical Journals**. Medical Journals are excellent sources of information. They present current opinions from the leading medical experts on various disease states and treatment options. The latest studies will be published in these journals. Ads for new and soon to be released products can also be found in these journals.

- **Specialists (M.D.s) involved in research**. In larger areas/cities, there are usually specialists involved in medical research. They will often be found at medical schools, but may also be out in the private practice area. These specialists are a great source of information. After all, they perform the testing and do the necessary research for new products. They know what will be available before anyone else outside the pharmaceutical industry.

Medical Community News.

In addition to medical information, there is always other news…personal news as well as professional news:

- **Hold shared, personal, information sacred!** As soon as you start to work in your territory, you will become knowledgeable about private/personal information. You are honor bound to keep such information private. Your reputation and credibility require that you protect the privacy of your customers and their patients. This doesn't mean that you should not report activity that you believe is harmful or illegal. This refers to keeping physician confidences. These are very often personal and have nothing to do with the practice of medicine.

- **Being tactful and considerate of your physicians requires more than polite behavior.** After you become a pharmaceutical sales representative, there are basic guidelines which sales representatives are expected to adhere to while in the field. Every company is different. Every pharmaceutical company will train their representatives and cover office etiquette with the representative. Basically, keeping in mind that the physicians' officesare like homes, places this situation in perspective. You wouldn't enter someone's home, rush to the back, hide, and pounce on the homeowner, would you? Of course not! While being assertive can pay huge dividends, being "pushy" can get you pushed out the door and told not to return. Learn the office environment; get to know the people before you decide which approach is best to gain time with the physician.

Attend Company Meetings.

Every company has different types of meetings that the pharmaceutical sales representative attends. These are:

- **POA Meetings**. POA means plan of action. These are the normal meetings that may be held at the district, regional, or national level. At these meetings the company will share with the representatives, what the marketing plan will be for the next three to four month period. *Certain product features and benefits will be the major focus for product marketing.* Features describe your product. Benefits explain the advantage of the product feature to the physician and the patient. Everything is explained in detail and everyone is taught to present the information correctly and effectively at these meetings.

- **National Meetings**. These meetings are held once a year or once every two years, depending upon the company. They are usually working meetings. Many will incorporate a POA with a new product launch meeting. Quite often, news about the company and achievement awards is on the agenda. These meetings present opportunities to network within the pharmaceutical company.

- **Regional/Bi-Regional Meetings**. These can be POA, product launch, achievement awards, etc. meetings just as the others can.

- **District Meetings**. Most POA meetings will be held at this level. Other special meetings will be called to meet the needs of the particular district to which you belong. While individual efforts are absolutely necessary for your personal success and the success of your district, region, and company, **teamwork is a key component to the district and company's success**.

- **President's Club/Circle Meetings**. These type meetings are usually reserved for award winners and are quite special. They are usually held in vacation settings. All expense paid trips for you and your significant other to beautiful places are part of the reward for a job well done.

- **Educational Meetings**. Not only are there opportunities to continue your education within the company, there are many opportunities outside your company. These include attending medical seminars, pharmaceutical representative meetings, speaker programs and various other meetings within the medical community.

- **Performance Meetings**. Generally these are one on one meetings with your district manager to assess your progress. These are very valuable meetings, because they highlight good performances, find areas for improvement and set future goals. Performance meetings are dedicated to helping the sales representatives achieve their highest potential.

Medical Meetings.

As an employee of a pharmaceutical company, you have to be present at various medical meetings. Supporting CE (continuing education) for physicians occurs in different ways:

- **Medical Society Meetings**. Pharmaceutical sales companies often call upon their sales representatives to attend medical meetings. At this type of meeting, representatives normally set up "displays." This is literally a display of current product literature and products. During breaks between listening to experts speak on current areas/problems in medicine, physicians will walk up to the displays to speak with representatives in order to gain current product information.

- **Dinner/Lunch Speaker Programs**. Usually, a representative will either ask a specialist in their territory or a specialist who speaks nationally to speak to a local medical society. The medical society and the district manager will have approved this. The representative will coordinate everything from speaker's fees and accommodations, program location guest list, dinner menu, to invitations.

- **Journal Club Meetings**. Sometimes the only way to see some busy hospital physicians, or perhaps even office-based physicians, is to get invited to journal club meetings. At these meetings, one physician (they take turns) will present a paper of interest to the group. The entire group will have a "brain storming" session. This is just another way that physicians keep up with current therapy in the medical field. Doing your homework and finding out who the members are, will help you know where to go to offer your assistance to the group. ***Remember that these are not pharmaceutical sales representative meetings!*** These are physicians' meetings. You must offer useful information if you are to be considered a valuable resource to the group. These meetings offer a great opportunity to develop rapport with important physicians.

Gain Formulary Acceptance.

In addition to calling on office-based physicians, it is very often necessary to call on pharmacy directors and clinical pharmacists in hospitals as well.

Most companies will have "Medical Specialists." These are experienced, "top-performing" pharmaceutical sales representatives who only work within hospitals and large clinics. Sometimes, there are areas where an "office-based" or "field" pharmaceutical sales representative can help the medical specialist. During product launches, in particular, extra help is needed to gain enough time with key people. Pharmacy directors, as well as key physicians determine whether your product is placed on the formulary at the hospital. If the product is on the formulary, then the physicians can prescribe it for their hospital patients. If the product isn't on the formulary, then the physicians can't prescribe it for their hospital patients without tremendous difficulty, or perhaps not at all. This is very important! It affects your ability to promote your product inside the hospital and outside the hospital. Product formulary acceptance usually takes teamwork.

Educational Meetings.

Not only do representatives attend the above-mentioned medical meetings, quite often they organize them. Physicians soon learn whom they can depend on for help. That person needs to be YOU! Even though this may sometimes be considered "above and beyond" your job description, the more helpful you are to your customers, the more they will appreciate your efforts. This brings many rewards. This can also gain you entrance to previously private areas of the physician's world. Representatives can be barred from many areas and this increases the difficulty of doing your job. Good communication skills and good problem solving skills can help ensure that you are one of the successful representatives who are welcome in areas where others are not.

Learning Programs.

Work with medical leaders. There are other types of learning programs such as teleconferences and audio conferences. Many hospitals enjoy having these educational programs for their physicians. This allows the physicians to earn CEUs (continuing education units) during a luncheon and there is no need for the physicians to take time off work. These programs are usually held in a conference room at the hospital. These "speaker programs" are set up so those physicians across the country can all attend without leaving their home, office or hospital. This can be especially helpful for the public hospital physicians.

Co-Promote Products.

Co-promotion of products within your company or with sales partners from other companies is very common. Sometimes two and even three sales forces within the same company will promote the same product. Sometimes two different companies join forces to promote products to increase coverage of their physician targets without hiring a new sales force. Each sales force will have different, or possibly identical goals. The representatives are given lists of targeted physicians and the names of their sales "partners" who share/overlap their territories. The reason pharmaceutical sales companies want several people calling on the same physician is that the physician will hear the sales message more often. Research indicates that the more the physician hears the message, the more likely he/she is to remember the message and "buy in" if the message is a good one. Research has shown that pharmaceutical sales companies sell much greater quantities of their products by utilizing this repetitive tactic. Representatives make an itinerary that is shared by the pharmaceutical sales partners so that the physician calls can be spaced appropriately. This prevents all the sales representatives who call on a certain physician from showing up the same week and even on the same day. This also allows the representatives to set up in-services and speaker programs as either joint or separate programs that do not interfere with their sales partner's activities.

Chapter

4

Networking

Pharmaceutical Sales Contacts.

How do you get to the person with the power to hire?

Who is the person with the power to hire and how do you get to that person? The person with the power to hire is the district manager. He may send you to a regional director for confirmation after you have been chosen, but that is usually just a formality. The district manager usually decides who will work in his district. There are different ways to get an audience with this person. They include:

- **Recommendation from one of his district sales representatives. This is the best recommendation!** Because the representatives' reputation is on the line, the representatives will not recommend anyone that they don't feel would make a good representative. Not only do they have to think about whether you have the potential to sell, but also whether you will "fit in" with the current sales team. *In order to achieve team goals, the team must be compatible.* District managers look at this as just as important as the selling skills. **Most pharmaceutical sales positions are never advertised!** Most positions are filled through pharmaceutical sales representative referrals. This is the **hidden job market!** Networking with pharmaceutical sales representatives allows you to compete with ten or fewer people for a position rather than hundreds or thousands of people when you apply for an advertised pharmaceutical sales position. Different pharmaceutical companies change their hiring philosophies and trends on a regular basis, but usually it is the district manager that determines who is hired.

- **Call back from district manager after receipt of your resume.** Any type of call back is great! That means your resume has sufficiently impressed the district manager and he is interested in meeting you. Since your goal is to get an interview with the district manager, you are doing great!

- **Call back from a professional recruiting agency.** Work with a professional pharmaceutical sales recruiter. Your competition will be greater when working with a recruiter than it is when working directly with a pharmaceutical sales representative but you will have much less competition with a recruiter than you will replying to national pharmaceutical sales ads. A call back from a professional recruiting agency is a strong positive. Recruiting agencies don't waste time on people who do not show promise. They live off of fees paid by companies who want to employ the best-qualified people available. The recruiting company's reputation is on the line every time they send an applicant to a district manager for an interview. Normally, the recruiter will narrow the applicants down to the top three if only one position must be filled. The applicants' resumes will then be evaluated by the district manager. He may or may not interview all three people. He will then choose one applicant to fill the position or he will decline all three applicants and the process begins again.

- **Respond to an advertisement for a pharmaceutical sales representative position.** When you see an ad in the newspaper, on the web, etc. should you apply? Of course! Don't miss any opportunities to gain an interview. Although your chance of gaining an interview this way is slim, it is certainly possible. Most ads will read that they want someone with one to two years of pharmaceutical sales experience. What if you don't have any sales experience? Apply anyway! Pharmaceutical companies and recruiters who place ads will always ask for what they would like to have. Why not? They would love to hire some great pharmaceutical sales representative who has two years of experience and a great sales history. That representative would be a proven sales leader. That representative would know the ropes and require little training. That representative could hit the ground running! In a dream world, representatives who match that criteria might line up for these interviews. However, in the real world, great representatives who have two years of sales experience are just getting really comfortable and are excelling at sales in their territories. They know all of their key physicians and their career paths are mapped out perfectly. They are making excellent money and are very happy where they are. They are in line for promotions, recognition, sales awards, fantastic trips and they aren't leaving! They are happy where they are! The only representatives who are leaving, in general, are those who aren't doing very well at their jobs or who have decided that this isn't the career for them. Those representatives who are leaving are frequently not the representatives that other pharmaceutical companies want to hire.

In the *Insider's Guide...* you will learn how to identify your own sales experiences even if you are not employed as a sales representative. Do you have experience persuading people to do what you have asked them to do? Can you persuade people to take the action that you recommend? Most people have some type of experience in this area.

This is selling! You just have to document and present this information correctly in order to be given credit for your experience.

Very often ads are placed by Human Resources Departments. The ads contain some general information including the required experience. The district manager who is attempting to fill a position may not even want to hire someone who has pharmaceutical sales experience. Hiring someone and having the company's training department teach that person to sell within company guidelines is sometimes preferable to the district manager. They prefer hiring inexperienced sales representatives rather than attempting to break "bad habits" or different sales techniques that a former pharmaceutical sales representative may have acquired during their tenure with another pharmaceutical company. **Remember, any company will hire the candidate who impresses them sufficiently whether that candidate has actual sales experience or not.** All of the pharmaceutical companies sales departments know that when they hire someone for an entry level pharmaceutical sales position, they are hiring "clay" that will be molded into the best pharmaceutical sales representative that the "clay" can produce. Don't let the wording in an ad discourage you!

- **Attend a job fair.** Pharmaceutical companies will place ads in local newspapers advertising a job fair. Sometimes, a local company or business will host the job fair and many different types of companies will be present soliciting applications for various jobs. There may be one or more pharmaceutical companies present. The participating companies will be listed on the job fair ad.

Going to job fairs and applying for positions is an excellent opportunity to gain an interview. At local job fairs you will not have as much competition as you will at national job sites. When you attend, just be certain that you dress like a pharmaceutical sales representative in a conservative suit and have at least ten unfolded copies of your resume to pass out prior to and during interviews. Have at least three copies of your matching list of references with you as well. You may interview several times with several different people from the same pharmaceutical company in one day. You must be prepared to answer questions! Study pharmaceutical sales questions and answers. You should practice selling products. Rehearse in front of a mirror and record your performance on videotape if possible. Research the pharmaceutical companies and know the names of their major products and the product indications. The worst-case scenario would be that you received some very good practice interviewing, but did not get chosen for a position.

Talk to Pharmacists, Physicians and Key Medical Personnel

It is always a good idea to find out how potential customers feel about the field that you've chosen. They can be wonderful sources of information. They can also give valuable insight into the specific perception of the pharmaceutical industry in your area. Do not ask only one or two people for an opinion. As in any situation, the more people you can consult with, the more accurate and balanced information you will gain about your chosen occupation.

Talk to Pharmaceutical Sales Representatives

Who would be better qualified to educate you on pharmaceutical sales than the ones who actually perform every day in that capacity? ***Pharmaceutical Sales Representatives can supply useful job information and they are the KEYS to entering the world of pharmaceutical sales.*** We will now cover how to find and get your foot in the door with these most important people.

Pharmaceutical Sales Representatives' Business Cards

Pharmacies/Physician offices:

Pharmacists are probably the best source of information concerning sales representatives in your area. Independent pharmacists are better candidates for information than those working in "chain" pharmacies. They can supply either business cards or names and numbers of representatives in the area. After you have completed your research on companies (see last chapter for list) that interest you, ask for contact information on the representatives from those companies. Physicians' offices may supply this information to you, but may not give the information out as readily. While you are unlikely to be granted time with a physician to ask for this information, do so if you have the opportunity. Many nurses and receptionists can supply the names of pharmaceutical representatives who call on their office and whom they like.

Key Medical Personnel:

Sometimes various hospital departments such as the hospital laboratory, heart cath lab, and central supply can get you in touch with pharmaceutical sales representatives. Be very careful how you approach these people. Do not violate hospital rules! Do not intrude uninvited! Getting kicked out of a hospital would not be a pleasant experience for you and it would seriously diminish your chance of gaining entrance to the hospital a second time. You must set up an appointment to see these people. If you have a friend who works in a hospital or nursing home, network with this person in order to gain access to a pharmaceutical sales representative.

Pharmaceutical/Medical Representative Societies:

Check your local phone book or ask your pharmacist or physician for the name, number, and contact person for the local pharmaceutical sales society. Another great place to find a list of pharmaceutical sales societies is at the *Pharmaceutical Representative* web site at www.medec.com/pr/.

Pharmaceutical Representative is a news magazine for pharmaceutical sales representatives. After you locate the local society, you can contact the society for information. Do not conduct all of the business on the phone! Attempt to set up a time to meet with a representative to get the information that you require. Attend a meeting if possible. Get your foot in the door as soon as possible! **These representatives are the keys to gaining a position in the pharmaceutical sales industry.** When companies advertise and you mail a resume in to them, yours may be one of 100,000 resumes. It's easy to get lost in the paperwork. A personal reference from a pharmaceutical representative gives you a tremendous advantage over all the other applicants!

Medical Conventions:

Every year there will be major medical conventions in all major cities. Local chapters of medical societies will have meetings. National medical society meetings will be held in the larger cities. At these medical conventions/meetings, pharmaceutical sales representatives from all major companies will be in attendance. They will set up booths filled with information. During breaks the physicians will visit the booths and receive information from the sales representatives. Because the medical convention costs are paid for primarily through educational grants from pharmaceutical companies, sales representatives from contributing pharmaceutical companies are allowed to set up booths and to speak with the physicians during breaks. The best time for you to speak with a pharmaceutical sales representative would be when the physicians are NOT present. Do not attempt to speak with a sales representative during the physicians' breaks because the representatives will be working during this time. If you interfere you will make a terrible impression upon everyone and you will be re-moved from the area. Be courteous AND smart. Wait until the sales representatives have finished speaking with physicians and are not busy to approach them.

How do you find out about these meetings? Ask a physician about any upcoming meetings. Ask a pharmaceutical sales representative about any meetings scheduled in the area. This will allow you the opportunity to meet many other pharmaceutical sales representatives. Inquire at all major hotels/convention centers about any upcoming medical society meetings.

Contacting Pharmaceutical Sales Representatives

Let's assume that you've acquired the names and phone numbers of some representatives. What do you do now?

- Call after 5:00PM if you have the representative's home phone number or beeper. Representatives are working out in their territories from 8:00-5:00 with the time varying from day to day. Be considerate. Ask if the representative has a few minutes to speak with you. Most will be working at their computers after they return home.

- Call anytime if you have the representative's voice mail number. Leave your name, number, and a brief message explaining your reason for calling. If the representative doesn't return your call within two days, call and leave another message. There are always meetings and time out of the territory that may result in a delay in the representative returning your call.

Setting Up Meetings With Pharmaceutical Sales Representatives

Don't agree to simply mail your resume to the representative! Offer to buy breakfast, lunch, or dinner to get to meet the representative. This is so important! When the representative agrees to this, you have overcome a major obstacle! In order for the representative to be impressed by you and ask the district manager to grant you an interview, the representative must have a good impression of you. Do whatever you have to do to gain a personal meeting with the representative; make the most of your opportunity when you meet with the representative. Show the representative that you have the skills necessary to be a good pharmaceutical sales representative. Be organized. Know pertinent information about the representative's company and products. Have several unfolded copies of your resume with you. Have letters of reference. Be prepared. This will turn into an interview whether it was planned that way by the pharmaceutical company representative or not. ***Be sure that you dress appropriately.*** This meeting will take place before, during, or just after business hours, so dress like a professional. Wear a suit. Tailored, dark clothes with white/pastel shirts or blouses suggest a business attitude. Make sure your shoes look as good as your suit does! Keep the "cool" clothes for outings with your friends.

When you meet with the pharmaceutical sales representative you will either gain a commitment from the representative for the field preceptorship or you will be denied the opportunity to have the field preceptorship. How would you turn either situation into a positive one for you?

1. Field Preceptorship Granted: Your day in the field will give you tremendous insight into the workday of a pharmaceutical field (territory) sales representative. **This is called a <u>Field Preceptor-ship</u> and after you complete your time in the field, be certain to list this on your resume.** You do not need to list the company that you completed the field preceptorship with on your resume but be prepared to share that information during an interview. Take the time to immediately write a "thank you" letter to the representative for allowing you to spend a day in the field observing the actual work involved in the job. Send a typed or neatly written personal note of thanks. Either letter of thanks would be acceptable. Make personal references to positive events that you may have witnessed during your day together. This will create a very positive impression with the pharmaceutical representative. Once again, you will be showing the representative that you possess the right qualities for employment in the pharmaceutical sales industry.

Do not ask endless questions of the representative! Show a real interest in the representative and the work that she is doing. It is quite all right to ask simple questions such as the following between calls:

- How did you gain your current position?
- How long have you worked for this company?
- What are your company's biggest products?
- What do you like best about your current position?
- Would you change anything about your job if you could?
- Can you describe a typical workday in the field?
- Which companies are your competitors? Which products?
- Do you know other representatives in the area that I might speak with about possible openings within their companies?
- Is there a local pharmaceutical sales representative society and how could I get invited to attend?
- Would you be willing to give my resume to your district manager ?
- Do you have any suggestions to help me pursue a pharmaceutical sales career?

At the end of the day, if the representative has time, you may then ask more questions without interfering with the representative's work. This will show the representative that you are a considerate person who values their time. That can only make you look good!

Why were you granted the field preceptorship? You impressed the pharmaceutical sales representative! You successfully "sold" yourself to the representative. Remember, the sales representative has incentive to attempt to find new talent for the company's sales force. Representatives who refer good candidates who are hired get "finder's fees" regardless of where the new hire is located within the company. District managers who interview good candidates who they cannot hire for their own territories pass the resumes of the good candidates on to other district managers for consideration on positions that they have open. Good pharmaceutical sales representatives can be difficult to find and when a district manager finds a good candidate, he does everything he can to see that person is hired by his company. The pharmaceutical company sales force is made up of teams of individuals and everything runs smoothly when everyone works as a team.

2. Field Preceptorship Not Granted: I have been getting more reports from customers about pharmaceutical companies refusing to allow anyone to "ride-a-long" with their sales representatives. There is no particular list of companies that will allow preceptorships prior to the interviewing process. The decision not to grant pre-interview preceptorships may be made at the national, regional, or district level within any company and this decision is subject to change.

Why would pharmaceutical companies decide not to allow their sales representatives to permit you to ride-a-long? The reasons are varied and they include but are not limited to the following:

- A non-company person repeated confidential information learned during a field preceptorship.
- A non-company person was injured during a traffic accident or at a physician's office during the field preceptorship and this has caused legal concerns for the pharmaceutical company.
- The company/district manager does not want the sales representative or physician distracted by the presence of a non-company person until and unless that person is a confirmed candidate for a pharmaceutical sales position within the company.
- The pharmaceutical sales representative doesn't want to help you or anyone else in the pursuit of a pharmaceutical sales position. This could be because the representative doesn't feel that she or he has the time to help you or this representative may not be the type of person who will help others. If this is the problem, just move on to the next pharmaceutical sales representative.
- The pharmaceutical sales representative simply is not sufficiently impressed with you so the field preceptorship is not granted. In this instance, you have a real problem to overcome.

How can you turn this situation into a positive experience and gain the necessary benefits?

- First of all, you have already gained a commitment from the sales representative to meet with you for breakfast, lunch, etc. That was your first major obstacle!

- You already have an excellent basic knowledge of a sales representatives job.
- Next you must ask smart questions and give smart answers in order to impress the representative and inspire this person to request an interview with the district manager. Use the information that you have learned from the *Insider's Guide to the World of Pharmaceutical Sales, 7ʰ Edition* to accomplish this task.
- Now is the time to use the career comparison information that you have created. Prove to the representative that you know what it takes to be a sales representative and that you have the knowledge and experience to be a great one!
- Basically, you must use this opportunity to sell the pharmaceutical sales representative on you and how you can be an asset to the company.
- If you have successfully "sold" the representative, that representative will see to it that you are

  granted an interview with the district manager. Don't expect to be given the district manager's telephone number. This is not likely to happen. Expect to be contacted by the district manager. Just remember to "ask for the business." Ask the representative if she or he is willing to recommend you to the district manager. If so, great! If not, ask what that reason might be because you want to do whatever it takes to gain the interview! When asked this way, you should get a truthful answer that will allow you to grow and improve your performance. Remember, you must accept any constructive criticism gracefully. That will make a good impression on the representative and may still result in an interview with the district manager!

"THANK YOU" LETTER

ALLISON THOMPSON

March 1, 2002

Joe Representative
100 Any Street, Apt. B
Any Town, Any City 10000

Dear Mr. Representative:

Thank you so much for allowing me to ride with you on February 28, 2002 to observe a real day in the life of a pharmaceutical sales representative. It is obvious that you have developed an excellent rapport with all of the physicians that we called upon that day.

Watching you go through the entire sales presentation from the opening statement to the close was a real pleasure for me. Reading about the sales presentation and then seeing it performed live was really amazing! I thoroughly enjoyed the experience. I am more convinced than ever that a pharmaceutical sales career would be the perfect career choice for me.

Thank you so much for forwarding my resume to your district manager for consideration for the new opening in your district. I appreciate the confidence you have shown in me. I will contact you in one week as you have requested if you or the district manager have not contacted me prior to this time. In the meantime, please do not hesitate to contact me if you need any additional information from me or have any additional information that you would like to share with me.

I look forward to speaking with you soon.

Sincerely,

Allison Thompson

8888 NORTH ROAD • NEW YORK NY • 00000
PHONE: 000.000.0000 • EMAIL: ALLEYTHOMP@NYNY.COM

Chapter 5

Resumes and Cover Letters

BASICS FOR RESUMES AND COVER LETTERS

Resumes are extremely important! They are an instant recap of the highlights of your education and work career. Make certain that there are no misspelled words and that your grammar is perfect. The style and length of your resume is also important. The style should be broken down into an outline format with limited essay. Place your name, address, phone number, and email address on your resume. List a specific objective as shown in the resume example. Do not be vague or wordy! Generalized objectives are very likely to result in the immediate elimination of your resume.

Include your "Field Preceptorship" near the beginning of your resume if you have completed one. This could be placed after your objective and before your work history information. This is very important because you are clearly highlighting that you have researched the position. Make the resume one page, two at the most…no longer!

If I had a preceptorship with one company and interviewed with another…should I still include the preceptorship on my resume even if it is with a different company?

Yes! Do not include specific information about the company that you completed the field preceptorship with on your resume. You can always convey that information during an interview unless you have specifically been asked not to do so. The person interviewing you should be very pleased that you have taken the initiative to learn about the industry. Most people will interview with several different pharmaceutical companies prior to being offered a position; so listing a preceptorship on your resume with one pharmaceutical company and interviewing with another pharmaceutical company is not unusual.

Do not include personal information such as marital status and age on your resume. Do not include personal references on your resume. You just need to provide the information that will capture the hiring manager's interest and win the interview. You will have many opportunities to explain the information you have outlined on your resume when asked during the interview.

Type your resume and print it on white or ivory paper. If your resume doesn't look professionally authored and presented then you will not "look" like a professional. Do not use brightly colored paper. Never fold your resume! Folded resumes are unattractive and project an "unprofessional" appearance. Pharmaceutical companies scan these resumes and folded resumes do not scan well. When mailing, you should place your resume in a cardboard-type mailer to protect it. If you need help formatting your resume there are options available. Microsoft Word has resume templates that are very easy to use. Just open up Word and then go to File and click on "New." Options will appear and you will click on "Other Documents." At this point you will see "Professional Resume," "Contemporary Resume," and a "Resume Wizard." You can use these templates to make your resume look professional. Appearance is very important!

- Remember that clerical people (or computers) very often scan resumes. These people/computers are looking for "keywords." These keywords would be: B.S. or B.A. degree, sales experience, sold, selling, sales awards, field preceptorship completed, member of honor society, school paper editor, community project organizer, managed, management experience, marketed, marketing experience, fund-raising experience, etc. Your resume must convey that you are a capable, motivated, achievement-oriented person. Use action words! If your Grade Point Average is above a 3.0, include this information with the degree. If your G.P.A. is less than a 3.0, do not list your score on the resume. **If the "scanners" do not see a four-year degree listed on your resume, you will be eliminated immediately!**

- **Always** include a cover letter unless you have been requested not to do so. Make sure the cover letter style matches your resume and that it is printed on matching paper. Never fold the cover letter! Do not list your current salary or salary history on your cover letter unless the company has specifically asked for this information. If you have to list salary information, list your total compensation, such as salary plus commissions and not just salary. Make the cover letter brief and to the point. Clearly state that you want the position, which has been advertised, and briefly cite appropriate education/experience, which would make you a good candidate for the position. Mention your contact within the company in the first part of the letter if you have one. Thank the hiring manager in advance for the opportunity to meet with him personally to discuss how you can be an asset to their organization. Paper clip your cover letter to your resume. Never staple the two together!

- Make copies of your resume and cover letter to take with you when you interview. **Have a copy of the cover letter that you mailed to the interviewing company with you when you interview.** In addition, have matching copies of your List of References, unfolded, with you to give to your interviewer at the appropriate time. Your List of

References should ideally contain three Professional References and three Personal References. Each reference should contain complete contact information including the name, company, address, telephone and fax if available. You will benefit if your references are easily reached.

Common Types of Resumes:

- **Chronological:** Most employers prefer this type of resume because the emphasis is on employment with the most recent employment listed first. If your strength lies in your work history and skills, then this format is a good one to choose.

- **Functional:** Employment is summarized or left off and skills and achievements are highlighted. This resume format allows you to highlight education and talents. This is a good format for the new college graduate with little or no work experience.

- **Combination:** Combines the Functional Resume and the Chronological Resume. Skills and accomplishments are listed first and employment history is listed last. This is the best format to use if your education, talents, and work history are equally balanced.

I have provided the most basic examples of resume format for instructional purposes. You may certainly use other formats. There are numerous free sources of information on the Internet with hundreds of examples of resumes. There are professional resume writers who can make the most of your work history and education information for a fee. Professional resume writing organizations are listed at the end of this chapter.

Please notice that you must highlight (outline) your qualifications simply and effectively. If your resume is too long or too wordy, it is not likely to be read or read in its' entirety. Remember, your resume is a "snapshot" of your education, talents, and work history. Make every word count! Your resume is designed to "get the interview" and not to "be the interview." Basic examples of all three types of resumes follow:

CHRONOLOGICAL RESUME EXAMPLE

000 Azalea Drive
Dallas, TX 00000
Phone: 214.000.0000
Fax: 214.000.0000
Email: susans@any.com

Susan Smith

OBJECTIVE   **Pharmaceutical Sales Job**

EXPERIENCE   2001-present   Hospital Health Center   Dallas, TX
Health Fitness Manager
•Sells and markets AAA Heart Rate Monitors.
•Increased Heart Rate Monitor sales in 2001 by 25% over year 2000.
•Conducts fitness assessments in a medical setting.
•Developed strong customer service skills through daily interaction with patients and physicians.
•Gained valuable computer and organizational skills through daily interaction with patients and physicians.
•Gained valuable computer and organizational skills through maintenance of company files.
•Increases communication skills and medical knowledge through preparation of treatment modalities and patient interviews.

March 6, 2002   ABC Pharmaceutical Company   Dallas, TX
Field Preceptorship
•Accompanied an experienced pharmaceutical sales representative for a day in the field to observe and gain knowledge of the daily activities of a pharmaceutical sales representative.

Honors, Awards, and Memberships
•National Dean's List, 2000
•National Fitness Council, 2000
•Red Cross Volunteer 1998-present

EDUCATION   December 2000   North Dallas University   Dallas, TX
•B.S. Exercise Fitness
•Graduated Summa Cum Laude

INTERESTS   Golf, Hockey and Computers

Functional Resume Example:
New College Graduate

Allison Thompson

Objective   Obtain a challenging pharmaceutical sales position that will utilize my proven communication skills.

Education   December 2001   New York University, New York
B.A. English, Minor in Writing
•Cumulative GPA: 3.9
•Major GPA: 4.0
•Dean's List
•Alpha Chi National College Honor Scholarship
•Golden Key National Honor Society
•Sigma Tau Delta English Honor Society

Key Skills

•Excellent Written and Oral Communication Skills
•Graphic and Web Design Skills
•PC and Mac Design Software

Experience

•Sold advertising to local businesses.
•Marketed Jazz Performances to local entites.
•Created promotional poster for NYU Vocal Jazz Group
•Designed and created Personal Web Site for multimedia course.
•Developed and sold business plan as class project.

Awards

•Academic Excellence Award 2001
•Presidential Scholarship, New York University 1997
•Poem Published in Ascent, 1996

Activities

•Vocal Jazz Performance
•Web and Graphic Design
•Urban Renewal Project Volunteer
•Freelance Writing

000 Any Road
New York NY 00000
Phone: 000-000-0000; Fax: 000-000-0000
Email: alleyt@any.com

Combination Resume Example

Jason D. Sallinger

OBJECTIVE   Pharmaceutical Sales Career

EXPERIENCE

- Generated a $300,000 increase in sales in 2001 over 2000 through cold calling and customer prospecting.
- Achieved the highest rating on Performance Assessment Evaluations for the last five consecutive years.
- Developed and implemented successful sales programs for new innovative technology program.
- Negotiated sales contracts resulting in excess of $1M during 2001.
- Knowledge of the following treatment areas: neuroscience, cardiovascular, urology and pulmonary.
- Experience in collaboration with other team members to bring projects to completion.
- Ten years of biotechnology sales experience that included hospital and institutional sales.
- Ten years of budget management and territory analysis experience.
- Developed and implemented successful hospital department sales presentations involving company approved, institution specific, research.
- Proficient with Microsoft Office 2000 and Photoshop.

EMPLOYMENT

10 years   ABC Biotech   Anytown, NJ
Hospital Equipment Sales Representative

EDUCATION

1990   New Jersey University   New Jersey, NJ
B.S. Biology; GPA 3.5

Email: jasons@any.com
000 Main Street, New Jersey, NJ 00000-0000
Phone: 000.000.0000; Fax: 000.000.0000

Cover Letters and Examples

Effective cover letters should have three basic parts:

- **Address.** Use a personalized address! Never send out "canned" cover letters. Always personalize your cover letter by including the address of the company to which you are applying. Additionally, personalize the salutation if possible rather than using Dear Sir/Madame.

- **Introduction.** The first line should be an "attention-getter." State the reason that you have sent your resume to the person. Let that person know that you are interested in the position that they are offering and let them know that you believe you are "perfect" for the position.

- **Additional listing of your skills and how you can benefit the employer.** Here is where you back up your "perfect" for the position claim with evidence. List your skills/education/ work experience and compare them to what the company requires to fill the position. Do not include negative information! Include salary information only if requested. The cover letter is the place for salary information when requested by the interviewing company. Never place salary information on your resume.

- **State what you would like to see happen.** State that you would like to talk with them in person about how you can be an asset to their company. Give them phone numbers and an email address so that they can easily reach you. Set a time limit. Tell them you await a response and will follow-up within a week to be certain that they have indeed received your resume. Just remember to be polite. It is possible to be assertive and still be polite!

Follow Up Letter and "Thank You" Notes

Never underestimate the power of a simple "thank you."

When you send a follow up letter or "thank you" note you are showing respect for your interviewer. The interviewer will not overlook the fact that you are a courteous person. Amazingly, most people do not take the time to add the final finishing touch to an interview, meeting, or preceptorship. Writing this letter also gives you an opportunity to prove that you have excellent written communication skills. The purpose of sending a "thank you" note is to accomplish the following goals:

- Show the interviewer respect and courtesy.
- Stand out in the crowd because you sent the "thank you" note.
- Recap briefly one main point from the interview that was very positive for you.
- Mention any additional helpful information that you may have forgotten during the interview.

Cover Letter Example

Susan Smith
000 Azalea Drive
Dallas, TX 00000
Phone: 214.000.0000
Mobile: 214.000.0000
Email: susans@any.com

March 1, 2002

Margaret Revere
ABC Pharmaceutical Company
1000 Any Street, Suite 300
Any Town, Any City 10000

Dear Ms. Revere:

Enclosed is a copy of my resume in response to your advertisement in the March 1, 2002 issue of the Dallas Morning News for a pharmaceutical sales position. With a solid record of tangible sales experience and proven sales performance, I believe I am very well qualified for the position. Please note that as a Health Fitness Manager, I increased heart monitor sales by 25% over the past year and had extensive interaction with the medical community. This constant contact with the medical community allowed me to develop excellent communication skills with physicians and other key medical community members.

Additionally, I have spent time observing a pharmaceutical sales representative at work calling on and presenting products to physicians. This has given me excellent insight into the daily job responsibilities of a pharmaceutical sales representative. My key areas of work responsibility closely match those of a pharmaceutical sales representative, so I am confident that I can excel at this position and contribute to the company's total sales.

My strengths are:
- Successful tangible goods sales experience.
- Excellent communication skills.
- Valuable organizational and computer skills.
- Knowledge of the pharmaceutical sales industry.

I look forward to discussing how I can be an asset to your company. I can be contacted by phone and email as listed above. I will follow-up with a phone call within the week to be certain that you have received my resume and to answer any questions you may have.

Thank you for your consideration.

Sincerely,

Susan Smith

Sample Cover Letter

February 24, 2002

Margaret Revere
ABC Pharmaceutical Company
1000 Any Street, Suite 300
Any Town, Any City 10000

Dear Ms. Revere:

Having recently received a Bachelor of Arts in English with a minor in Writing, I am eager to initiate a pharmaceutical sales career at ABC Pharmaceutical Company. My personal philosophy, which is evidenced in the accompanying resume, is one that emphasizes a strong work ethic and a commitment to excellence in all facets of life. I am particularly skilled in the areas of written and oral communication and have the ability to utilize those skills in an efficient and accurate manner. These talents, in combination with the attention to detail exhibited in my work and the ability to effectively and creatively resolve multiple issues through an analytical approach, place me in the position of being able to contribute significantly to ABC Pharmaceutical Company in the position of pharmaceutical sales representative.

In addition to this, I am certain that my extensive base of software knowledge and excellent interpersonal skills, would allow me to perform well in all of the varied pharmaceutical sales job responsibilities, while acquiring the industry knowledge necessary to further improve my contribution to the collective goals of the company. I am eager to discuss with you the many ways in which I may contribute to the continued success of your organization.

My resume is attached for your consideration.

Sincerely,

Allison Thompson

000 ANY ROAD • NEW YORK NY • 00000
PHONE: 000.000.0000 • EMAIL: ALLEYT@ANY.COM

Sample Cover Letter

Jason D. Sallinger

March 5, 2002

Margaret Revere
ABC Pharmaceutical Company
1000 Any Street, Suite 300
Any Town, Any City 10000

Dear Ms. Revere:

Attached is a copy of my resume in response to your on-line posting of the following position:

JOB TITLE: US-NJ-PHARMACEUTICAL SALES POSITION

With ten years of hospital equipment sales experience, I believe I am qualified for this position.

Highlights of my work experience and strengths include:

- Experienced biotechnology sales professional.
- Proven sales leader. Generated a sales increase of 300K during 2001.
- Innovative and creative. Developed and successfully implemented new sales program.
- Team player.
- Achieved highest Performance Assessment Evaluation.

I look forward to discussing with you how I can meet your needs for the pharmaceutical sales position and can be reached by phone, fax or email as indicated on my cover letter and resume.

Thank you for your consideration.

Sincerely,

Jason D. Sallinger

000 MAIN STREET • NEW JERSEY, NJ • 00000-0000
PHONE: (000) 000-0000 • FAX: (0003) 000-0000
EMAIL: JASONS@ANY.COM

FOLLOW UP LETTER

Allison Thompson

March 1, 2004

Margaret Revere
ABC Pharmaceutical Company
1000 Any Street, Suite 300
Any City, Any State 10000

Dear Ms. Revere:

Thank you for allowing me to interview with ABC Newspaper Company. I appreciated the opportunity to meet with you and present my qualifications in person.

You stated that pharmaceutical sales is a very rewarding as well as challenging career and it takes a special personality to cope with this career. I believe that my proven ability to work under pressure and meet deadlines as an individual and as a team member will transfer nicely to a pharmaceutical sales career. My advertising experience combined with excellent written and oral communication skills would allow me to become a productive member of the news team immediately.

I look forward to speaking with you again soon.

Sincerely,

Allison Thompson

000 Any Road * New York NY * 00000
Phone: 000.000.0000 * Email: alleyt@any.com

Need More Help With Resumes and Cover Letters?

Do you feel confident in your ability to write an outstanding resume and cover letter now? Do you feel that you may need the services of a professional resume writer? If so, you should easily find a qualified resume writer through the following listed organizations.

It is very important that the resume writer you choose be a Professional Resume Writer. It is even more important that the resume writer has **experience preparing sales resumes and pharmaceutical sales resumes** in particular. The following organizations can help you choose the perfect resume writer to create that very important pharmaceutical sales career resume. If you contact one of these four associations, be certain that you interview the resume writer and ascertain what percentage of this writer's resumes are written for sales professionals and for pharmaceutical sales in particular. It is critical to employ a writer with the appropriate type of experience.

Career Masters Institute (CMI) - cminstitute.com - 800-881-9972
National Resume Writers' Association (NRWA) -nrwa.com — 888-NRWA-444
Professional Association of Resume Writers (PARW) - 800-822-7279
Professional Resume Writing & Research Association (PRWRA) - prwra.com - 800-225-8688.

If you contact one of these four associations, be certain that you interview the resume writer and ascertain what percentage of this writer's resumes are written for sales professionals and for pharmaceutical sales professionals in particular. It is critical to employ a writer with the appropriate type of experience.

..

Chapter 6

One of The Chosen Few

After You Meet The Right People

Moving forward.

You've met the right people. You've made contact with representatives and you now have a recommendation from at least one of them. What do you do now? This section covers making the most of your networking and "Sending the Right Message." This will help you determine which employer will be the right one for you and how to stack the odds for employment in your favor. Now you will have to do a little personal research because only you will know which company matches your personal and professional needs. I can help you know which questions should be asked and answered.

Professional Contacts

You've made them...now make the most of them.

Winning plan. After you've met some representatives and you feel that you have their vote of confidence (and even if you don't), you need to learn everything you can about the company from the representative. I am not talking about clinical research here. You can always pull up company statistics and I cover that later. Here we are interested in the "attitude" of the company. Is the company "forward thinking?" Is the company proactive or reactive? What are the real opportunities for personal and professional growth within the company? How does the current representative see the company as compared to the industry? How does the quality of products (product industry rank) compare to the competition? Do they carry unique products or is this a "me-too" company?

"Me-too" simply means that the product is in the same class as many others and works the same way. These products require a different selling approach from unique products. They can be more difficult to sell. How does the current representative feel as a person within this company? Does the company take good care of its' employees?

Your Reputation

Make sure it is the best one.

Keep in mind that your reputation will follow you everywhere you go for the rest of your life. Be aware that pharmaceutical companies will investigate anyone that they intend to hire to see if they can detect any character flaws or potential problems. They will check your driving record. Speeding tickets won't automatically get you disqualified but it doesn't look good. You have to be able to drive a company car. They will talk to your college advisor, your best friend, and your minister to find out more about your personality and character. **Do whatever you need to do to make sure that the reports will be good.**

How to ensure good reports.

Make sure that you let all persons that you may have used, as references, know that you have done so. (You will have asked their permission to use them as references first!) Do this in advance. Tell them that you are attempting to gain employment in the pharmaceutical field and that pharmaceutical companies do thorough background checks. This doesn't mean that you need to tell people what to say. It's just easier for people to think through what they will say when called if they have advance notice.

Sending the Right Message

Consistent Behavior

Always be consistent! Consistency gives the perception of a person in control; one who knows what she's doing. A consistent person is organized. Consistent people have their lives together. They know where they've been and where they're going. This is the right message to send in any area of business, and this is certainly true for sales.

Professionalism

Being professional is a planned position. You must dress and conduct yourself like a professional.

- **Dress professionally.** Dark tailored business suits are best for interviews. White/pastel shirts/blouses are best. Your outfit should be perfectly coordinated, spotlessly clean and perfectly pressed. Men and women alike should make sure that their shoes are clean and polished. The nicest suit in the world will not look right with unclean/unpolished shoes! A district manager actually told me that he automatically eliminated any interviewee who arrived with unpolished shoes. Men should wear conservative silk ties. Ladies should wear dress suits, not pant suits, for interviews. Ladies, keep the jewelry low-key. Do not wear dangle or hoop earrings. Simple hairstyles are best. Wear light makeup. Do not wear bright eye shadow or brightly colored lipstick. The interviewer must be able to "see" a professional who cares about the statement that their appearance makes to others. Dressing for success isn't just a cliché. It really does make a difference to those who see you. You must always look like a professional!

- **Be professional.** The nicest business clothes in the world won't help you if your actions don't match your attire. Project self-assurance, not arrogance. Be friendly, engaging, and project a healthy energy level. Smile and greet your interviewer with direct eye contact and
a warm, firm handshake. Pharmaceutical companies are looking for self-starters who know their business and know how to communicate with others.

Create Your Own Luck!

Set yourself up for success.

- Do whatever it takes to prepare yourself for the position that you want.
- Get the correct education and work experience that you need to qualify for the job.
- Make the right contacts and then make the most of them.

Be Prepared.

Organize.

Showing an ability to organize everything will score major points with any interviewer. They know that in order to perform well as a pharmaceutical sales representative, you must be able to organize everything from your paperwork, sales calls, and time to your personal life.

Set goals.

Pharmaceutical companies love people who set goals. Goals are necessary for optimum achievement. Have a checkoff list of the things you have to do in order to get to your interview and another list of things you need to do to get through the day of your interview. List the things that you would like to accomplish. These are your goals. ***Know where you would like to be in five years, seven or ten years...etc.***

Prioritize.

Know what the number one priority is in the pharmaceutical sales industry. **The number one priority is "selling the product!"** Other areas are very important, but nothing else matters if the product doesn't sell.

Don't Give Up!

If it's worth doing...
Have notes or examples that serve as "proof-sources" to confirm that you are tenacious! If plan A doesn't work, go to plan B, to C…through the entire alphabet if necessary to achieve your goal. Sales representatives have to be creative and tenacious to get the job done.

Preparation Through Work Experience

Increase your chance for success.

Knowing what kind of work experience is most valued by the pharmaceutical industry gives you an edge. Find part-time or full-time work in a sales position to help prepare you for a sales position in pharmaceutical sales.

Regardless of what type sales experience you have, make it good experience. The more awards you can earn, the better you will look to your future employer. They are looking for achievers. They want sales
leaders who are independent thinkers and those people who can also work as part of a team.

Best type of work experience.

The best type of sales experience is one where you sell tangible goods. This may be shoes, jewelry, or computers. Selling computers, software, and electronics are excellent means of getting the right kind of sales experience. A basic knowledge of computers is highly desirable, if not necessary, to be hired by a pharmaceutical sales company.

Chapter

7

Selecting The Right Company

Research.

By now you have made some contacts in the pharmaceutical industry and you have an idea about which company may be a good match for you. While you can always apply to the top ten or twenty companies, you should consider everything that you have learned from the representatives, pharmacists, and physicians. The next step will be to look at specific information on the companies that look like a good match for you from your contact information.

Where are they based?

Do your homework! Know where your potential employer is based. In how many countries have they established a base? Learn everything you can about the company. How did they get started? When did they get started? Are there any unusual stories there? Remember, all pharmaceutical companies have a parent company in one country. They place bases in other countries as well. For example, Merck's corporate home is based in the United States but Merck has bases in numerous other countries. Most pharmaceutical companies have parent companies located somewhere in Europe. They all have bases in the United States, Canada, Australia, etc. Hiring practices, interviews, etc., are basically the same all over because the same types of people are needed to sell the products.

What are their products?

Know their newest products by name! Know the indications of these products. Know what disease states they're used to treat in general. No one expects you to be an expert on a product, but if the company makes a drug that treats asthma, know that. You can look up information on products at your local library and on the Internet. Most products will be listed in the PDR, "Physician's Desk

Reference," except the very newest ones. Information on the newest products can be found on the Internet under the product name or under the producing company's name. Medical school libraries are also excellent sources of information on pharmaceutical products, pharmaceutical companies and pharmaceutical product studies. Some companies specialize in respiratory, cardiac, or psychiatric drugs. Know this information about your future employer. This lets them know that you are truly interested in their company and their products, not just the compensation package that they offer.

What is their growth history?

Knowing their growth history will help determine whether they are a stable viable company. Good growth trends suggest a good product pipeline. The better the pipeline, the more stable the company. **Companies who fit this criterion should provide more job security and more opportunities for professional growth.**

What is the company's size?

There are positives and negatives related to small and large size companies. A small company may be new and provide tremendous potential for professional advancement. A "family" environment is common in small companies. However, the company may be small because the product pipeline is small, or the products themselves are merely "me-too" products. They may not have their own research center and scientists to create new products. Management may not be strong within this company and that could be why the company continues to have slow growth or no growth. Large companies very often have good product pipelines. Growth is impossible without a good product line. Strong product pipelines are excellent indicators of a good management team. The "family" atmosphere tends to be lost in the large companies, but there may be even more opportunities for career advancement because of increased production and growth. These are factors that must be considered when deciding which company would be a good match with your personality. Very often large companies are more willing to hire new college graduates and train them than are smaller companies. Smaller companies do not have the budget available to train people that larger companies do. Therefore, based on your sales experience or lack there of, you should consider this when selecting companies for potential employers.

Employee ratings and Industry rankings.

How do the employees feel about their employer? This information is best acquired from your new representative contacts, pharmacists and physicians. Of course, you will want to target a company who looks after its sales force. Some companies place more value on their sales force than others. Some appreciate well-trained sales professionals, while others feel sales representatives are easily replaced. You may have to read between the lines somewhat to get this information from the representative.

There are rankings available, which rank companies according to size, professional society involvement, continuing education, and professionalism. This information should be used in addition to other information to determine which companies appear to be compatible with your personality and sales ability. All this information should be available to you on the Internet. You need to research only those companies that you have chosen as potentially compatible employers. Companies who have won outstanding awards will certainly post this on their web sites. That makes your job as "researcher" easier.

Chapter

8

Pharmaceutical Company Requirements

You must be able to answer all the questions in this section before you start the interview process. Take your time and carefully consider your answers.

Attitude

Attitude is everything.

A positive attitude is an absolute necessity. Pharmaceutical companies look for confident, highly motivated, self-starters. Being a team player is also essential to success. Show a willingness to "do whatever it takes." If you are mobile, let them know that. That's part of "doing whatever it takes." How is your *attitude?*

Ability

Ability to do the job.

- Do you have good communication/ interpersonal skills?

    Can you communicate effectively? Great communication skills are a must if one is to have a successful career as a pharmaceutical sales representative. Interpreting body language as well as the spoken language, analyzing the information and responding appropriately, are key "must have" skills for pharmaceutical selling.

- Do you have a "return on investment" mentality?

Do you invest your time and effort in a manner that will produce the maximum benefit from the use of your time? It's almost like investing in the stock market. You must research and analyze your potential investment in order to determine whether you will earn a sufficient return on your investment. When calling on physicians you must determine which physicians have the greatest potential to write your product. Next you must determine who already writes your product. You use this information to determine where you spend your time. Why? You want to get the greatest return on your time and sample investment.

- Are you organized in every area?

How do you plan your days? Do you create lists in order to organize and prioritize your day? In order to perform well in a pharmaceutical sales position, you must be extremely well organized. That is the key to making the most out of your time and to reducing stress. If you aren't organized and you rush from place to place you will probably create problems for yourself and you will not accomplish your goals. One of the keys to being a successful pharmaceutical sales representative is by working **smart** rather than hard.

- Can you accept leadership?

Can you accept guidance and constructive criticism as well as positive re-enforcement? A key responsibility of the district manager is to coach and guide his sales team. This is a responsibility that he has to the company and his sales team. Everyone learns through mistakes. A good manager will use constructive criticism in order to help you learn from your mistakes and reach your highest potential as a pharmaceutical sales representative.

- Are you a problem-solver?

Can you take a difficult situation, find a solution, and resolve problems? Pharmaceutical sales representatives work as problem solvers every day. When the physician treats a patient for a disease, he is attempting to solve the problems or adverse effects on the patient that are associated with the disease. As a pharmaceutical sales representative you will constantly be calling upon physicians and offering solutions to the adverse effects of disease upon patients in the form of drug therapy and information. **Your job is to help the physician help his patients.**

- Do you have good negotiating skills?

Can you get what you need while giving the customer what he needs and wants? This translates into creating "win-win" situations. Everyone is happy when everyone wins. You must always approach the pharmaceutical sales job from this perspective. You are successful only when you consistently negotiate well and create "win-win" results.

Loyalty

How loyal are you to your employer?

Your employer will expect complete loyalty from you as will any employer. You will prove your loyalty in several ways:

- Always defend your company to others unless there are extreme circumstances where this would be legally or morally prohibitive.

  Defend your company's reputation. The company's reputation is linked directly to your reputation. Report any defamation of the company to your district manager who will make sure the right company officials are aware of any potential problems. Never criticize your employer. They hired you! Do your best work for them because they issue your paycheck.

- Keep company information confidential.

  Never reveal company secrets. When a pharmaceutical company hires you, you will probably be asked to sign a "non-compete" document and will definitely be asked to sign a confidentiality document. Why? Pharmaceutical companies reveal confidential information on studies and products prior to public release. Confidential trademark and research information must not be allowed to reach competitors who may use this information to advance their position to your detriment.

- Report competitive action/information to your company.

  Always keep your company abreast of what is going on in your territory. You are the eyes and ears of your company.

- Stay with your employer through bad times as well as good times whenever possible.

  The pharmaceutical company who has hired you has given you a tremendous opportunity to have a professional career where you can earn a very nice salary, have an opportunity for upward mobility, have on-going access to continuing education, and an opportunity to retire with a good income. Pharmaceutical companies spend a tremendous amount of money on training their sales forces. They invest heavily in their staff. This should always be remembered and taken into consideration by you when you make career decisions.

Dedication

- Are you willing to work overtime to achieve your sales goals?

Some days you will be required to work past 5:00PM. Some physicians will see you only after 5:00 and 6:00PM. Additionally, there are often evening speaker programs, or dinner programs that you must attend.

- Are you willing to work extra time planning your activity?

In order to truly maximize your time, you must make pre-call and post-call notes. When you do this, you always know what information you covered with the physician and how the physician responded. You also have a plan of action for your next call based on your post-call note.

- Are you prepared to focus on your goals until they are achieved?

You must be tenacious to be an effective pharmaceutical sales representative. Every day you will have to overcome resistance from physician office personnel and from the physicians themselves in order to perform your job. It takes a tenacious person to continue to plan, show up at the office, and call on physicians who repeatedly turn you away.

Creative Thinker/Problem Solver

- Do you like problem solving?

You absolutely must enjoy problem solving and puzzles in order to really enjoy a pharmaceutical sales job.

- How creative are you at solving problems?

Good sales representatives create solutions for prescribers of difficult patients everyday. They give good information that helps the physicians choose the correct medication to treat the patients' disease states.

- Do you approach problems with the realization that there are almost always many different ways to resolve problems?

Thinking outside the box is necessary in order to grow as a pharmaceutical sales representative. Does the fact that something hasn't been done mean that it can't be done? Of course not! It simply means that no one else has done it. All problems have solutions. It just takes a little time and effort to find a solution.

- Can you use analogies effectively?

Effective sales presentations often incorporate analogies. "Just as this product is safe for use in the elderly, diabetic patient, because of its great renal profile, it is also safe for use in the dialysis patient for the same reason." You must constantly and consistently be able to compare patient types, patient disease states, and treatment modalities.

- Are you good at demonstrating your ideas? How good are you at "show and tell?"

Pharmaceutical sales representatives are masters at "show and tell." Everyday, pharmaceutical representatives use visuals, study aids, studies and items to "show" the physician information while they "tell" the physician about their product.

Tenacity

- Can you push forward in the face of resistance?

Rejection is an everyday occurrence in the life of a pharmaceutical sales representative. Everyday, receptionist, nurses, and physicians will attempt to prevent you from speaking with the physicians. Are they doing this just to be mean? Of course not! Physicians' offices are very busy places. Remember, the physician's first priority is the patient. It is not seeing sales representatives. Being tactful, considerate, and a good resource will help the pharmaceutical sales representative overcome the common resistance factors.

- Can you set goals and then pursue them over extended periods of time?

Pharmaceutical sales representatives set short term and long-term goals as part of their plan of action. It takes perseverance to continue to pursue a long-term goal that is difficult to reach, especially when you do not see any type of immediate result. Pharmaceutical selling is known as "consultative" selling. It is not considered "hard sales." Therefore, it can take months to start to see the results of your work. Pharmaceutical selling requires patience as well as persistence.

- Can you keep your enthusiasm and persevere when things don't go as planned?

People (physician's office personnel) will prevent your best-laid plans from working at times. How do you cope with this? Pharmaceutical sales representatives have to be **flexible**. If you had a 9:00AM appointment with a physician and it is cancelled at 8:55AM because the physician has too many "work-ins" or "had to go to the hospital," etc. then how do you deal with this? This is an everyday occurrence in pharmaceutical selling. You always have a plan B in the event that plan A doesn't work. This prevents frustration and wasted time.

- Are you undaunted by a setback?

How do you cope with failure? Do you see failure as a learning experience? Does it just mean that you didn't do enough research? Did you fail to plan for all objections to your message? You must view setbacks as temporary. The setback is not a permanent problem. You just regroup, prepare well, and go back and get the job done.

- Can you walk back into a situation where you felt uncomfortable?

Pharmaceutical sales representatives do this daily! It's just part of the job. Sometimes the physicians are stressed out or rushed and they may be abrupt, and at times, even rude. What you must realize is that everyone has bad days. We all do. Sometimes, we say things we shouldn't and we regret it. The next time you walk into the office, the physician will probably be having a good day and may not even remember causing you discomfort. That's just part of the human factor in the pharmaceutical sales job.

- Can you push yourself beyond your comfort zone?

How can you grow personally and professionally if you don't take chances and extend yourself? While you never violate company policy and procedure, pharmaceutical companies are great at encouraging and empowering their pharmaceutical sales representatives to be creative. It is through new and innovative ideas that pharmaceutical companies and pharmaceutical sales representatives remain competitive.

Professionalism

- Is your conduct always above reproach?

Never give anyone reason to complain about your behavior. There is no excuse for bad behavior.

- Do you retain your control when others do not?

Your actions are totally within your control regardless of what other people may say or do. You never have to lower yourself to a substandard level of conduct.

- Do you always present a calm, confident presence?

Calm and confident people exude self-assurance and an air of authority. This helps build your customer's confidence and gives you credibility.

- Are you always prepared to present your product information?

Being prepared to present your product information is a major part of a pharmaceutical sales representatives job. If the representative prepares pre-call and post-call notes and keeps up with all company learning programs and instructions, the representative will always be prepared.

- Do you "look" like a professional? Are you dressed for business?

There's no excuse not to dress like a professional. This is the easy part. Don't take your appearance for granted because it matters. Remember, you must always take great care to present yourself as a professional. Dressing like a professional is just one part of the total professional image package.

- Do you always represent your company in the best possible manner?

Never lose sight of the fact that your reputation is completely intertwined with that of your company. In the eyes of your customers and in the eyes of the general public, you **are** the company. Don't ever do anything that would reflect negatively upon your company or yourself. This means that your private and public life must never reflect negatively upon the company.

Chapter

9

Interview Preparation

Know the Company.

In recapping what we listed earlier, know as much as you possibly can about the company. This will show the interviewer that you are interested in that company. While it would not be appropriate to "trash" any other company, feel free to state what you like about the company interviewing you. Everyone likes to feel special! While you may be happy to get any position in the pharmaceutical industry, the interviewing company should feel that they've been chosen by you because you are impressed with them. Any interesting company history you may have uncovered will help you show your interest in their company. **Having a copy of the information that you have compiled on the interviewing company to show the district manager during an interview will win some major points for you!** The neater, more organized your report is, the better you will look. Have copies of product advertisements from medical journals such as the *New England Journal of Medicine,* or the *Journal of the American Medical Association.* Any interviewer will be impressed with the fact that you have done your homework and have prepared for the interview. **They want people who are prepared to present their materials!** Pharmaceutical sales representatives excel at this! They do their research, study, and prepare for their calls upon physicians.

Prepare A Company Presentation Binder.

Your company research binder should be filled with neatly typed and organized information that you have compiled from the information that you found researching the company. You should not just print web pages and place them in your binder unless they look nice and you intend to use them as "proof sources." You should include information such as:

- Company's major products.
- Company's major areas of research or expertise.
- Special Awards won by the Company.
- Name of Chief Executive Officer.
- Address of parent company and of United States base.
- Total company sales.
- Total company Research and Development Expenditures.

Know The Products.

Knowing the current products that the company is promoting shows that you are up to date on important company information. Just a basic knowledge is all you could be reasonably expected to have. Just know the product name and what the indication is for the drug. **If their product is #1, that's a good thing to mention!**

Know The Management Style.

Any information that you know regarding the personality and management style of the district manager will certainly be helpful now. District Managers usually have approximately ten representatives working under their supervision. If the position is located within the same district as your new representative friend's, you have a tremendous edge. You will be seen as a serious applicant with hiring potential simply because one of his representatives has recommended you for the position. While *you certainly would not repeat anything* that the representative may have shared with you, this recently gained knowledge can be used to help you prepare for the interview questions.

Knowing the district manager's personality style will help you predict his management style. One type of information that pharmaceutical sales companies teach their new hires during initial training is to learn how to recognize distinctive personality traits so that the new hire can apply this information when working with physicians. **There are four basic personality types that you will encounter while calling on physicians and these four basic personality types apply to all humans, including the district manager who is interviewing you!** These four basic personality types are:

- **Thinker**: To earn the trust of a thinker you must be thorough, comprehensive, accurate, organized, logical, knowledgeable, use proof sources, and most definitely know the facts about the information you are presenting.

- **Feeler**: To earn the trust of a feeler you must be honest, personable, maintain eye contact, show a genuine interest in the person, and have a "non-salesperson" manner. You must be warm and friendly. You must talk with them about how their peers feel about the information you have presented, and how using this information helps people. Feelers enjoy casual conversations.

- **Sensor**: To earn trust with a sensor, you must have a direct, "to-the-point" approach. You cannot vacillate. You must state your main points briefly and clearly. Avoid being wordy. In other words, just "net it out" or get to the point and get there quickly! Be confident, but do not be pushy. This will win the sensor's respect. Sensors are serious people. Sensors tend to be turned off by emotional comments. Sensors are very punctual. Sensors like to hear both sides of a story, good and bad.

- **Intuitor**: To earn trust with an intuitor you have to "show and tell." Demonstrate the latest and the best, the most innovative way to do or accomplish whatever you are discussing. Be forward looking. Make the conversation exciting. Intuitors like personable people just like feelers do. Intuitors are innovative thinkers. They look to the future. The more word pictures you paint, the more metaphors you use with an intuitor, the better the impression you will make.

Understand The Different Types of Interviews.

The pharmaceutical companies are using "different" types of interview formats. A popular one is called the STAR format. It is very similar to the sales presentation outline. There are several variations of this selling standard with different acronyms but there is no significant difference between the formats.
STAR stands for:

- <u>Situation</u> (goal, opportunity or situation)
- <u>Task</u> (What is your plan of action for accomplishing your goal?)
- <u>Action</u> (What did you actually do to accomplish your goal?)
- <u>Result</u> (What was the specific result of your action?)

An example of how you could answer an interview question using this format would be:

Question: What is your greatest achievement?

Answer:
- **Situation (Opportunity):** Gain a contract with the largest HMO in my territory.
- **Task:** Convince the Buyer/Pharmacy Director that my product offers the most cost-effective efficacious therapy for his patients.
- **Action:** Devised a power point presentation outlining the features and benefits of my products to show that I had the most cost-effective efficacious product for his patients. Presented this information to the buyer/pharmacy director. All information was backed up with proof sources, my cost data, and information from their own database.
- **Result:** Convinced the buyer/pharmacy director that I had the most cost-effective, efficacious product for his patients and I won the contract!

Remember, there are a limited number of questions that the interviewer can ask. Because of this, the companies keep trying to "reword" questions so that they appear to be different questions. The same is true for interviewing formats. Pharmaceutical consultants are constantly trying to create "new methods" for asking questions in order to better assess the pharmaceutical sales candidate's ability and potential . They present the formats and questions as "new ideas" and "new questions" when it's really just the same ideas and questions worded to sound differently. The pharmaceutical companies are just attempting to improve their interview process so that they don't make costly hiring mistakes.

There is no real difference between this type of interview format and the interview formats that these companies have been using. This type of interview format has also been called "situational." Just practice outlining your answers in the above format and you will be able to answer the questions efficiently and effectively.

Telephone Interview:

Telephone interviews are screening interviews. They may be conducted by someone from the pharmaceutical company, by a recruiter hired by the pharmaceutical company, or by a computer. These interviews are extremely unpredictable. Be prepared for questions that are designed to determine your true personality. Are you a "team player" or are you independent? They will word these questions so that you will probably feel that you should answer it with the independent answer but a "team player" answer is usually best. You may only be given 15 seconds to respond. This is a deliberate attempt on the company's part to get a true response from you.

If you are lucky enough to gain a telephone interview with a person, expect to explain why you believe that you will be a good pharmaceutical sales representative. Be certain that you tell them that you love selling and you love a challenge. Think about instances where you "sold" someone on your idea, etc. Did you create a new program at school that you talked everyone else into supporting? That would be selling. You could start your sentence with a comparison statement. "Just as pharmaceutical sales representatives call on physicians and talk them into writing prescriptions for their products, I..." You can also mention selling situations where you were successful in the sales job that you had. Don't volunteer information about how many people worked for the company unless this is advantageous to you.

Screening Interview:

Screening interviews are designed to reduce the number of qualified candidates for a position. This is accomplished by creating interview questions that will eliminate those candidates who are generally qualified on paper but who do not have the right personality for the job. All candidates are asked the same set of questions. You may be given only 5-15 seconds to respond. Usually the questions are "yes" and "no" questions, or "one answer" questions. A rigid scoring system is built into the test and the individual's circumstances are not considered. These screening interviews are usually conducted by telephone, but may also be conducted by mail and even in person. Computers and human resources personnel usually conduct these interviews. Screening interviews are usually brief. Fifteen minutes is the normal time frame but some may last twenty minutes.

During the last three years I have received many reports from customers stating that they were being asked six "situational" questions during telephone interviews. All this means is that the interviewer will present you with a "situation" and you must tell them how you would respond. They're just using the STAR interview format. For example, the "situation" could be that the physician just told you that he isn't going to write prescriptions for your product because he writes for the competitive product and he really likes it. What do you do? The answer can be found in the interview section of this guide. It really doesn't matter how they phrase and rephrase the questions. They can't ask you a question that you can't answer if you have done your homework and learned all of the information in the "Insider's Guide…."

Second Interview:

Only serious candidates are asked back for a second interview or a "real" interview. With the exception of those times when companies are adding new sales forces, normally twelve or fewer people will be called back for a second interview after the screening. At this point, district managers, field sales trainers, and management trainees will interview you. This time the questions will be more specific and more difficult to answer. All of the questions will require thought and detailed information from you. You will definitely need to know your *Insider's Guide* interview question and answer section here! Be certain that you state at the beginning of each interview that you want the position. This lets the district manager know that you don't mind "asking for the business." You can then "show and tell" the district manager the information that you have gathered on the company and how impressed you are with the company. State how impressed you were with the pharmaceutical sales representative and how much you enjoyed your day in the field with that representative. Sum it all up with a comment about how all of this information helped you decide that their pharmaceutical company is the right one for you!

At least one pharmaceutical company has been surprising the interviewees by telling them that they will be taking a pharmacology test as part of the interview process! Yes, it's a test! Only serious candidates are given the test. First, the candidate is given a book to take home and study in order to prepare for the test. There is no need to panic or go out and buy pharmacology books. First of all, the information that you will need to know for the test will be specific and limited in its scope. All you need to study is the information that will be made available to you by the district manager. You will confuse and overly stress yourself if you attempt to learn what others have spent a lifetime learning if you approach this "assignment" incorrectly by studying pharmacology books. By studying the information that you are given, you can concentrate on the information that you have to know and understand to pass the test.

Why would the pharmaceutical company decide to administer a pharmacology test? This is a sure way for the pharmaceutical company to determine BEFORE they hire you that you are capable of learning the type of information that you need to know in order to sell the products successfully.

Third, Fourth, Fifth, and Even Sixth Interview!

Don't allow anyone to convince you that three interviews is some type of magic number and that a decision is made at that time! By the time you reach the third interview, six candidates may still be competing for the position. As you can imagine, the questions will become more difficult. You should know the interview questions and answers section well enough to answer the questions easily and smoothly when they are asked! At this point in the interview process, all of the candidates are good candidates. Now they are attempting to zero in on the small differences between candidates that would make one candidate superior to the other candidates for a specific territory. This is the interview where the questions you asked the representative that you had the field preceptorship with can save you from being eliminated. **Do you remember what the rep said about the district managers' personality and how the rep described the "personality" of the district?** The district manager doesn't just want a good representative who can sell products; he wants a person who will mesh well with the rest of his district. This is very important because everyone must work together on common goals to be successful.

When the district manager has narrowed his choice down to one or two candidates, the regional director usually interviews the candidate(s) also. The regional director will normally agree with the district manager's judgment but occasionally, he may not agree with the district manager on a candidate. Normally if the district manager has told you that you are his candidate for the position, meeting with the regional director is a mere formality and is usually a nice experience.

Prepare A Personal Presentation Binder

Prepare a complete personal presentation ("proof sources") binder as well as a company research binder.

Part of this personal presentation binder will contain your resume, references, and "proof sources" such as college transcripts and sales awards. You should also add the following to your personal binder:

- **Sit down and analyze your job experience** and make a list comparing what you do to what a pharmaceutical sales representative does. Just look at the information from the Insider's Guide concerning what a sales representative does and then find something comparable within your experience to compare. If you do not have any work experience, compare some of your college course work projects to what a pharmaceutical sales representative does.

- **Create a "career-comparison" document** on your computer and have a side-by-side comparison (two columns) of your job responsibilities and that of a pharmaceutical sales representative prepared for the district manager. Remember to write brief, clear, descriptions in the columns. Do not make the "career comparison" document too long. Just make it neat and professional in appearance. It should match your resume, cover letter, and recommendations in format, style, and paper. You will impress the interviewer when you do this. Many of my customers have reported that using their personal presentation binder made all the difference and won the job for them. **This can turn a screening interview into a major interview, so be prepared for this! See "career-comparison" example:**

Allison Thompson

Pharmaceutical Sales Representative	College Courses/Advertising Job
Calls on health care providers through preset appointments and through "cold calls."	Calls on advertising business customers through appointments and "cold calls."
Presents company-approved sales presentations to physicians and other key medical personnel.	Presented successful sales presentations to customers resulting in numerous sales contracts.
Plans and organizes daily activity within designated sales territory for maximum efficiency through the use of a call planner and territory analysis.	Maximized daily activity through careful planning, targeting and scheduling of appointments.
Maintains knowledge of company and competitor's products.	
Stays current on medical research developments.	
Stays current on medical community news.	
Represents company at medical meetings.	
Attends company meetings.	
Works on a sales team to co-promote products within company and with company partners.	
Enters all call activity into a company provided computer program every day.	
Tracks Performance Management Data for use in Performance Management Evaluations.	
Maintains Sample Storage and Inventory.	
Works on special assigned projects with district manager approval.	

Give Them What They Want.

This may sound like something you would not want to do, but think before you make that decision. This does not mean you are doing anything wrong. Don't ever do anything illegal, immoral, or even questionable! This means that the interviewer will have a set of questions, which may have been prepared, by an outside source. Certain answers will be anticipated. Certain answers will be considered correct, or appropriate, for someone seeking a sales position. Throughout this guide, I have been teaching you the basics that pharmaceutical companies expect from you. I have attempted to let you know what they want. As with any employer, you have to deliver a pleasing performance. *In many ways, your interview will be a performance.*

How To Turn A Negative Into A Positive.

Remember that even though most questions will be designed to test your knowledge of sales and to assess your potential to succeed in this area, **there may be one or two questions designed to elicit a negative response from you.** Be prepared to turn a negative into a positive. If you have anything in your background that could possibly be considered a negative by the interviewer, be prepared to handle questions about it. Think about how you have learned from an experience; maybe you have even become a better, more empathetic person because of your experience. **Resist the temptation to place blame on anyone else!** Take responsibility for your actions. Perhaps you are stronger, wiser and more determined because of something unfortunate, which has happened to you. Then you can give an example or two to support what you have said. Always try to have "proof-sources" of some type. Interviewers will be impressed if you have something in writing to prove anything that you might say. "Proof-sources" are usually something in writing, which proves that what you are saying is true. After you become a pharmaceutical sales representative, you will use "proof-sources" in the form of studies and journal articles on a daily basis to prove the truthfulness of your statements about your products to physicians. Using "proof-sources" during your interview can help you win the position.

Understand the new Marketing Code adopted by PhRMA.

The Pharmaceutical Research and Manufacturers of America (PhRMA) voluntarily adopted a new marketing code that governs the pharmaceutical industry's relationships with physicians and other health care professionals. This marketing code went into effect July 1, 2002. Most pharmaceutical companies in the United States voluntarily implemented the new code guidelines prior to this effective date. Basically, the code states that meals provided for physicians/health care professionals must be modest and in connection with informational presentations. Items given to the physicians must be modest and/or must provide a primary benefit to the patients. These health care practice-related items should not cost in excess of $100. Entertainment may not be provided to the health care professionals/physicians.

This action has been taken to avoid the appearance of impropriety and the potential undue influence of monetary items on health care professionals. The new code is actually very beneficial for the pharmaceutical sales representatives. **This has leveled the playing field.** All pharmaceutical sales representatives will have equal opportunities to meet with physicians and present their product information. This can only benefit the talented pharmaceutical sales representatives. Now whether you work for a large company with major resources or you work for a small company with limited resources, you have an equal opportunity to sell your company's products and have a very successful career.

Chapter

10

Interview
Questions & Answers

First of all let's concentrate on legal and illegal questions. *You should not be asked illegal questions by a professional pharmaceutical company representative*, but illegal questions are asked occasionally. Illegal questions may be asked through ignorance or failure to word a question properly.

Illegal questions include but are not limited to the following:

- Age
- Marital status
- Family questions
- Country of Origin
- Religion
- Sexual Preference
- Health Status
- Political affiliations

However, there are exceptions to the rules for illegal questions whenever the question is job-related. For example, in order to perform a pharmaceutical sales representative's job you need to be able to lift forty pounds. Questions relating to this may be asked but should only be asked of those candidates chosen for the position. You will also be asked about your driving record if you are considered for the position. Why? Pharmaceutical Sales Representatives drive company cars and must have good driving records.

There are legal personal questions. They are:

- Have you ever been convicted of a crime?
- Are you eligible to work in the U.S. and do you have documentation to prove this?
- Can you perform the essential job functions with reasonable accommodation? This question can only be asked if they show you a job description.

How would you handle an illegal question? You should always deal with the concern behind the question. For example, if you are asked whether you have children or plan to have children, you should address the real concern hidden within the question. What the interviewer really wants to know is whether you will be able to travel and spend the time you need to spend away from home in order to get your job done. Do not point out to the interviewer that he is asking an illegal question! As a general rule you should just ignore the fact that you have been asked an illegal question unless there is a pattern of illegal questions. Now let's move on to the recent pharmaceutical sales interview questions.

Recent Pharmaceutical Sales Interview Questions:

1. Why did you decide pharmaceutical sales would be the right career for you?

This is the most basic of questions, but you are almost certain to be asked this question. While people interviewing for other types of positions are asked why they decided on their career choice, it is very important that you answer this question correctly for a pharmaceutical sales interview.

- **First tell them that you love selling** and site examples where you have done this even if you haven't been employed as a salesperson. Mention instances where you persuaded someone to "buy in" to your ideas, etc. That is selling! Mention that you have always been highly motivated, energetic, and enthusiastic. Successful sales people have all of these qualities as well as being creative and resourceful. Be prepared to cite examples where you displayed these behavioral characteristics.

- **Next, expound upon why pharmaceutical sales would be right for you.** This is a good time to pull out the information that you have collected during your research. You can explain how stable the industry is, how exciting it would be to be part of such a dynamic field, and one where the opportunity to help thousands of people is a reality. State that this would give you tremendous job satisfaction. Also let them know that you realize the opportunities for personal and professional growth are tremendous with pharmaceutical sales companies. You will thrive on the daily challenges of performing a pharmaceutical sales representatives job. (This would be a great time to mention the "field preceptorship" and how much you enjoyed your day in the representative's territory!) The research you have done on their company and the industry, and the extra effort you have put forth to spend a day in the field to see for yourself what a pharmaceutical sales representative does will give you tremendous credibility. You will be viewed as a serious candidate!

2. What is your current occupation?

Give an honest answer, but highlight any area of responsibility that you may have which would be seen as a benefit for someone in pharmaceutical sales. This would be a good time to show the "Career Comparison" information that you have placed in your Personal Presentation Binder. You will have already compared your job responsibilities to that of a pharmaceutical sales representative. Were you responsible for marketing a product or idea to others? Have you analyzed a "buyer" to determine that buyer's potential? Do you have daily contact with physicians or other medical personnel in your day-to-day activities? These are excellent job responsibility areas to compare with pharmaceutical sales job responsibilities. Be careful not to make a negative statement. Always expect to be asked to prove any statement that you make!

3. I see you have held several different positions over the last five years? Can you explain why?

The obvious objective in this question is to determine whether you are a "job-hopper." Training and educating pharmaceutical sales representatives is very time-consuming and expensive. A bad choice would yield an ineffective pharmaceutical sales representative and one that would potentially leave the job "undone" because that person has again decided to do something else. The district manager will attempt to ascertain whether you are a dependable person and whether you do indeed really want a career that offers upward mobility. He must be convinced that you will stay and work smart. If you have changed positions in order to increase the challenge of your job and allow upward mobility, then that is an excellent reason for changing jobs. Career transitions or job transitions made to increase compensation for your work is another good reason.

4. When did you decide to pursue a pharmaceutical sales career position?

You might reply that after your extensive research into this career field including actually going on a field preceptorship, that you believe this a perfect career for you. Then you must explain why it is perfect for you. It is perfect because you thrive on the type of challenges faced by pharmaceutical sales representatives! You want to make a difference at a job you are certain you will love. Pharmaceutical sales is a perfect match for your personality and work experience. Then supply proof for your statement.

5. How long having you been seeking employment in the pharmaceutical sales industry?

Your answer here will be important. You have the opportunity to make yourself look good with the right answer. If you have been looking for a position for a long time, six months or more, then you need to present yourself as a tenacious person who never gives up because you are absolutely certain that you are the right person for the job. Whether you have been granted interviews will matter, because the district manager will wonder why you didn't gain the position if you interviewed. On the other hand, if you didn't gain an interview that means you failed the first sales test. Perhaps you turned a position down because of location. That's a good reason to decline. If you've just started looking for a pharmaceutical sales position and you've already gained interviews, it's because you are impressive, on paper and in person.

6. How does your current or former job experience compare to pharmaceutical sales?

Use the information in the career comparison document that you have created. This will show a side-by-side listing of your job skills and experience compared to those of a pharmaceutical sales representative.

7. What was your rating on your last Performance Management Review?

Most people will have some standard type of performance review with a rating system. For example, your rating system may be 1-5 with 5 being best. Perhaps you rated a 4 which is better than average. Now's the time to "show and tell." Pull a copy of your last performance review out of your
briefcase, attaché, etc. and show the district manager your overall rating. You could show him the areas where you excelled and those areas where you worked and improved your performance. The
district manager wants someone who is capable of accepting leadership and working on areas of weakness while maximizing areas of strength. He's just using another source for identifying your strengths and weaknesses.

8. How would you describe "selling?"

Selling is persuading someone to agree with you and to buy whatever your product happens to be.

9. How would you describe the best boss you've ever had?

He's still trying to get some insight into your personality and how you respond to different management styles. Telling him what you like about your favorite boss tells him much about you. Your input gives him insight into what type of management you've had, what you're used to, and how you respond. Knowing that you like having your boss involved and that he's a good mentor tells the current district manager that you are "teachable." Also stating that you enjoyed the freedom of being empowered to excel at your current position while knowing that you can count on your boss for advice and support when you need it makes you look good. You were always treated fairly and had the necessary materials to perform your job responsibilities.

10. What is your salary with ABC Company?

First you should attempt to avoid a discussion of salary if at all possible because you don't want to give them a low salary that will cause them to offer you a low salary in return. On the other hand, if your salary is too high, they may not think that you would take the position, so they won't waste more time on you. Try stating that you've heard only serious applicants who are being considered for the position are asked questions about their salaries. Look thrilled and ask if this is indeed the case! If the interviewer states that this is premature, just state that you "had to ask." This will come across as asking for the business because that is precisely what you have just done. If he still wants an answer about the salary, you will have to give him one. Be honest, but don't shortchange yourself. Add your commissions, bonuses, etc. and give him your total yearly compensation.

11. If you had only one word to describe yourself, what would that word be?

There are a number of one-word answers that would be correct. For example, if you say, "creative" that is a correct answer. Just be prepared to prove how and where you have been "creative" through the telling of some story or event that happened in your life or better yet, show pictures and tell. If you created something great and received an award for your creativity, show your picture, medal, etc. You could also use, "dependable," "energetic," "competent," "competitive," "enthusiastic," etc. Just use the keywords that describe characteristics of pharmaceutical sales representatives.

12. What do you consider your greatest strength?

Use words that describe what they want in a representative. These would be self-starter, self-motivated, creative, flexible, confident, tenacious, team player, tireless worker, energetic, enthusiastic, positive, and an "overwhelming desire to succeed," etc. "I never give up!" Be prepared to give an example of a time when you successfully reached your goal by not giving up on your goal in the face of resistance or hardship.

13. What do you consider your greatest weakness?

Your "weakness" must always be a "strength!" You may be a self-described "workaholic." Maybe your "weakness" is your tenacity. You may be so tenacious that you just don't give up easily. You just can't help yourself!

14. What is your greatest achievement in the area of sales?

While it is usually not a great idea to "toot your own horn," in most types of interviews, feel free to do just that! Tell them about any awards that you have won and pull out the documentation to prove it. **They love to see people use proof sources!** That is an important part of a pharmaceutical sales representative's job.

15. Have you ever had to correct or compensate for an incompetent boss?

Be ever so careful with this question! They want people who can take constructive criticism and who will be "team players." The best answer would be "no." If you have been fortunate to have a good manager, do not hesitate to say so. They will ask what you thought made that manager such a good manager. Answers like, "He had a wonderful way of suggesting ideas or methods to work with difficult clients, or ways to improve my reports, ways to help me gain more sales," etc. are good answers. ***Do not show any resentment of management!*** Just state that management is necessary and desirable, because management gives guidance that helps you do your job better.

16. What do you feel is more important, an achievement of monetary value or the feeling of being the best, the feeling of accomplishment?

The feeling of accomplishment is always best…the knowledge that you have done your best and that you met your goal. Sometimes, this allows you to be "recognized as the best" and to receive a "monetary award" because you are the best and that is a wonderful bonus!

17. Why should we hire you over other candidates?

This is a difficult question. How do you sell yourself now? This is another opportunity to make you look great. You should have either a sense of what the district manager is looking for in a candidate by the time you get this question or he may have already given you the answer based on the questions that he has asked of you. Asking him what he's looking for in the ideal representative at this point would be foolish because you would appear to be evading the question. You need to ask early in the interview when you have the right moment what he is looking for in a representative. It's always good to state, "I can do the best job because," and then list your reasons and back them up with some type of proof source. Use the information that you have already been given by the district manager when he explained what he wants to see in a pharmaceutical sales representative. Not only are you giving him back the answer he has already supplied, you're doing it the way a real pharmaceutical sales representative would. You're using proof sources!

18. Name five reasons why you feel you would make a good pharmaceutical sales representative.

- "I can sell, as evidenced by…(show proof source)"
- Pharmaceutical sales offers a lucrative, challenging, rewarding career and I thrive in that type of environment.
- My marketing (health care, pharmacy, nursing, etc.) experience will enhance my ability to communicate with the key decision makers and allow me to make my mark as a first-class salesperson. I don't mind giving 110% because the rewards are there. The more I sell for the company, the more I sell for my district and myself!
- I've always wanted to help people and pharmaceutical sales presents the perfect opportunity to do this.
- I have a proven ability to learn and communicate technical information as evidenced by…(show proof source).
- I managed X number of people (or maybe a geographical territory) during my employment with xyz corporation. I can apply this management and analysis experience to my pharmaceutical sales territory, etc.

19. How can you be sure that you will excel at a pharmaceutical sales career?

Now's the time to emphasize that you have succeeded at every career endeavor! You set goals and then you attain them. Perhaps you're a new college graduate. You chose your major. You persevered and you made the grade. You follow-through on whatever you start. You don't quit! Ask the district manager if these qualities are some of the qualities that the best pharmaceutical sales representatives have. He will have to agree.

20. Do you know people who can vouch for your character or competence on the job?

Have your typed List of References with you. Give the district manager a copy at this time and invite him to check your references. Tell him that you are confident that he will be pleased with the feedback that he will receive from your references.

21. If I call all of the people on your list of references, which words will they use to describe you?

This question is designed to yield information that will give the district manager insight into your personality. He knows that you are only going to give him references that are favorable to you so that's a given. What he wants to know is: What type of person are you? When people start to describe themselves, they normally reveal character strengths and character weaknesses. Always describe yourself using keywords that describe pharmaceutical sales representatives.

22. Have you interviewed with other companies?

If you have, admit it. You never know who knows whom. He may be best friends with the guy who interviewed you last week. Just restate your interest in the profession and your intense desire to become part of it. Anyone who is very interested in gaining a position will do his or her best to get an interview! That means interviewing with as many companies as you can. You want to be hired by the current district manager because his company is #1 on your list. Be prepared to tell him why his company is #1 with you.

23. How do you feel about working on your own most of the time?

State that you look forward to the challenge. Give examples of how you currently "work on your own" whenever possible. Explain that you are goal-oriented and love a challenge. Cite examples where you have set goals and achieved them on your own because you were motivated. Use the words self-motivated. Use the phrase "team player" and explain how the team doesn't always have to be intact to be a team. Everyone carries their load and works together, though separately, for the common good.

24. Why did you choose the college major that you chose?

Think about this and how you can apply your course work to a pharmaceutical sales career! Use the information that you have learned in the "Insider's Guide…" to determine how you can apply what you have learned in your major or minor area of study to a pharmaceutical sales career.

25. How do you think that your college course work will help you with a pharmaceutical sales career?

Think about your major and minor areas of study. What basic skills have you learned that can be used in a pharmaceutical selling career? For example: The person who holds a bachelor's degree in English will have become skilled in the art of written and verbal communication. That person would have been required to read massive amounts of information and then write a paper or create an "outline" of the important information. That takes organization and research. A pharmaceutical sales representative must possess these skills.

26. You may be given a hypothetical situation and asked to "sell" the interviewer something. If this happens, be sure you give features and benefits of the "product" which you have been asked to sell and **ASK FOR THE BUSINESS!**

Features are qualities that the product has. Example: The pen has a slim design with two flat surfaces.

Benefits are examples of how the features will benefit the user of the pen. Example: The slim design and flat surface allows the customer to hold the pen easily and securely, thus making writing easier and more enjoyable.

You must then probe for acceptance to see if you have earned the right to ask for the business. Is there any reason why he wouldn't want to write with this pen? If not, then ask for a commitment to buy some pens and ask how many pens he would like to order today. For in-depth sales information see the SELL ME SOMETHING directive, question # 130.

27. Why do you want to work for our company?

Show them or refer to the research you have done on their company. Point out what you like about the company and why. Let them know that you consider them a leader in their field and that you would be proud to work for such a respected pharmaceutical sales organization. Mention their great product pipeline and how this makes the company secure. Mention that this also allows many opportunities for professional growth.

28. What kind of income do you expect to earn during your first year as a pharmaceutical sales representative?

Be optimistic but don't go overboard with this answer. You know what an average starting salary is for a pharmaceutical sales representative. Most new representatives can expect to earn about $50,000 in salary and commissions the first year. Some will earn more. Just state that you intend to be in the top 25% of sales representatives during your first year because you will learn everything that the company will teach you about selling and then you will apply that knowledge to the best of your ability. You are confident that armed with the proper information and sales training, you can accomplish your goal.

29. Tell me what you like about your current manager's style of management?

Make all positive comments. List everything that the manager does that you believe shows good management skills. Mention the guidance, the great working atmosphere that allows you to ask questions freely, the constructive criticism that really doesn't feel like criticism because he's so good at teaching by example.

30. Would you change anything about your current manager's style of management?

I hope you can truthfully state that you think he does a fantastic job and you really like the way he motivates his team. If not, think of something very small and insignificant that he does or does not do. Maybe you would have liked faster feedback on your weekly field reports, but that's really all you can think of that you would change.

31. Why do you want to leave your current profession?

Don't say anything negative! Just mention that you want increased responsibility and a greater challenge, opportunities for upward mobility, and the opportunity to increase your earnings.

32. What do you like about your present job? What do you dislike about it?

When stating what you like, mention things that are also part of the pharmaceutical sales job, even if they are general things. The dislike part could just be a lack of opportunity for personal and professional growth. Do not get personal with your comments.

33. Do you feel valued in your current position?

Perhaps you feel valued at your current position but you realize that the opportunity to grow in your current position is limited. Perhaps there is no upward mobility because the company is small, or profits are down. Either way, that translates into limited opportunities and you know you can contribute more and would welcome the opportunity to do so.

34. What are your current job responsibilities?

Explain your responsibilities and tie any similarities that you can to the pharmaceutical sales job. You should be well prepared for this question if you have already prepared a "career comparison" document.

35. Does your current employer empower you to perform your job to the maximum of your potential? How are you empowered?

This is the "how would you like to be managed" and "what's your current work environment like" question again. You answer will say much about whether you accept authority, perform as a team player or act as a renegade. The ideal answer here would be one where you are empowered to be creative and to perform your job to the best of your ability where your strengths can be emphasized. While this is all within company guidelines, you have latitude to explore new ways of getting the business.

36. What motivates you to go to work everyday?

It takes a special kind of person to get up, go out, and make cold calls in addition to keeping set appointments knowing that she will face rejection throughout the entire day. Stating that you love the thrill of knowing that you have persuaded someone who may have been adamantly opposed to your point of view to accept your point of view and act upon your suggestion is excellent! There is such a tremendous sense of satisfaction when you know that you have delivered your message and you overcame all objections and made the sell. That means you have actually changed someone's mind or used your knowledge and persuasive skills to influence someone. It's a tremendous high! You are goal-oriented and it feels good to reach those goals. That is why you try and try again until you reach your goals.

37. How do you think you rank in your current position as compared to others in that position?

Now is the time to say that you've won sales awards, etc. and back it up with proof sources. Remember that they love to see you use proof sources! If there are no sales awards, state your rank in your current position with an explanation of the ranking system if necessary. New college graduates could state their class rank and list performance awards received.

38. Tell me why you believe a pharmaceutical sales career would be more rewarding for you than your current job?

Perhaps you do not really have the opportunity to make a difference in people's lives in your current position. With a pharmaceutical sales career you would. Perhaps there is no real opportunity for upward mobility with your current position. With a pharmaceutical sales career there are many opportunities to move up and learn new jobs within the pharmaceutical industry.

39. How long would you like to work as a pharmaceutical field sales representative before being promoted into another position?

Some people want to work and retire as a pharmaceutical sales field or territory representative. If that's how you feel it is quite all right to say so. If you want to learn about the industry from the ground up and work your way up in the company that is great too. After becoming hired as a pharmaceutical territory representative, you should expect to work at least two years in that position before becoming eligible for other positions.

40. How do you feel about working past 5:00PM?

Just say that you believe that work ends when the job gets done, and that doesn't always happen by 5:00PM.

41. Would you be available to work evenings some time?

The answer is YES! Let them know that you are flexible and understand that some time must be spent attending speaker programs, etc. because this is a great opportunity to increase your product sales.

42. Tell me which pharmaceutical sales responsibility you would like least?

Make sure your answer to this question is not a major part of the pharmaceutical sales job! It can't be calling on physicians and selling the product. It must be something minor such as writing a weekly report. Maybe you just don't enjoy the writing part as much because you would rather be selling. However, you understand why it is necessary and you always perform your duties in any position even if they aren't your favorite.

43. Are you free to travel to other states for a week or more at a time?

You will have to travel from time to time. You will have to attend training classes and company meetings. If this is a problem, you could be disqualified at this point. You need to think about how you will handle any possible problems you may have with travel and have a solution before you interview.

44. If we hire you, where do you see yourself in five years, ten years, etc.?

Have an outline of where you would like to be as an employee of their company. You may have listed three years of general field sales. Attend training class for the medical specialist position. Promotion to medical specialist in three to five years would not be unreasonable. Maybe at five to ten years you would expect to have an opportunity to apply for the district manager position. You must decide what your short and long term career goals are before your interview.

45. If we hired you on the spot today and you started working for us tomorrow, where would you see yourself in six months?

No one expects to be asked where he or she will be in a short period of time such as six months. The goal of the interviewer is to catch you off guard and see how you respond. You could reply that in six months you expect to have successfully completed all of the following:

- Initial Sales Training Program.
- Called on all of the physicians in your territory several times each. You could be very ambitious and say 5-6 times each.
- Have your territory well organized and under control.
- Set up and completed "lunch and learn" programs as well as "speaker programs."
- Started to see the impact of your sales presentations through an increase in sales in your territory.
- Be a contributing member to your sales district and company.

46. What are your expectations of our company? What do you want from us?

You expect an exciting, challenging, rewarding sales career opportunity with the best sales training available. You expect to be given all the sales aides and materials available to help you perform at your best. You expect the best management and guidance to help you reach your goal of becoming a top performing pharmaceutical sales representative.

47. What does competitiveness mean to you?

Competitiveness just means challenging. Sales people challenge themselves every day. You go out and make your sales calls and challenge yourself to do the best job you've ever done. When you compete with other people, and you will, the goal is to be the best at whatever the challenge is at that time. You will always be in competition with your competitors who sell products that compete with your products. However, you will also compete with other sales representatives within your own company for rank, recognition, and rewards. Competing allows you to be the best you can be and keeps you sharp. It ensures that you always perform at your best because the grading system is always in place. It's the best type of motivation. Although bronze and silver medals are admirable, you always strive for the gold.

48. Rate yourself on a scale of 1-10 with 1 being most and 10 least competitive.

Since you have to be competitive to succeed you need to rank yourself as being #1 in this category. It's the thrill of winning and the tremendous sense of accomplishment that fuels you.

49. How competitive are you?

This is the same question. They have just rephrased it. As I stated earlier in the book, there are a limited number of questions that the pharmaceutical companies can ask to ascertain whether you are pharmaceutical sales material. Therefore, they keep rephrasing the same questions hoping to get you to reveal more information about yourself that will help them make hiring decisions.

50. How can you reconcile competitiveness and being a team player?

This is a very tough question! Sales people by nature are very competitive. How do they function well as part of team when all of the individual members of the team must compete for rankings, recognition and awards?

The true team player realizes that in order for the team to be successful, the big picture must be the focus. Offering help and creative ideas to other team members must be part of the plan of action if your team is to win over the competition. Some people may think that this will reduce their chance of winning the #1 slot, but it really shouldn't. Being a team player and sharing information just forces you to perform to the very best of your ability. When everyone has the same information and the same "edge" then it comes down to your sales performance. That will determine who is really best. True sales professionals are not intimidated by their roles as team members. They welcome the challenge.

51. Name a time when you failed to make the sale? How do you think that sales call could have been handled differently from the way you handled it?

Think of a time when you failed to make a sale and list the reasons why you failed. Perhaps you did not prepare well enough for your call on some specialist. Because you did not prepare well, you could not overcome his objections. What did you learn? Never take any sales call for granted! Always prepare extensively for each call. Identify your objective. Identify and list the possible objections. Then prepare your response to each and practice using your proof sources to overcome the objections.

Stating that you really learned a valuable lesson that has made you a better sales person will score points for you. Tell them how you went back with proper preparation and succeeded. This will tell them that you learn from your mistakes and that you get the job done.

52. What do you think a pharmaceutical representative's job is?

A pharmaceutical sales representative's job is to sell his company's products and represent his company in a professional manner at all times, in all places.

53. Outline a day in the life of a pharmaceutical representative.

Pharmaceutical representatives meet with physicians through preset appointments and through "cold" calls (no appointment). During these calls, the representative will present information on their specific product following the guidelines established and approved by their employer. On an average day a pharmaceutical sales representative will present their product to 8-10 "office-based" and/or "hospital-based" physicians. The representative will also average two (2) pharmacy calls (sales presentations to pharmacists) per day. In some territories the "office-based" representative will also average one (1) hospital call (sales presentations to physicians, key medical personnel, and pharmacists) per day.

54. How do pharmaceutical sales representatives sell products to physicians?

Pharmaceutical sales representatives sell their products to physicians through product presentations by persuading the physicians to write prescriptions for their products.

Product presentations are the primary responsibility in a pharmaceutical sales representative's job description. During a product presentation a pharmaceutical representative will:

- Open a product discussion by making an attention-getting statement or asking a question.
- Describe or paint word pictures of patient types and disease states so that the physician will identify with the presentation message.
- Explain how your medication will benefit the patient AND the physician.
- Supply an indication, mechanism of action, contraindications, side effects, and dosing information on the product.
- Overcome objections or simply supply additional information through the use of proof sources such as medical studies and visual aids.
- Present cost-effectiveness and therapeutic advantage information. This is important and a concept that has proven very effective over the past several years as compared to just covering efficacy and side effects as was emphasized in the past.
- Ask for the business and gain a commitment from the physician to write prescriptions and/or start patients on the product with samples supplied by you.
- Follow-up on all sales calls with another sales call with the goal of advancing the sale every time.

55. Which part of the pharmaceutical sales representative's job do you think is the greatest challenge and why do you think this?

Depending on which district manager asks the question, the answer can vary. Most would agree that it is one of the following two things:

- **Gaining quality time with the physician.** Gaining quality time with the physician is not getting a signature and dropping samples. In order to succeed in gaining quality time, you have to gain the physician's attention and interest. You also have to get the physician to "open up" and let his guard down in order to really hear and accept the information that you present. Quality calls may last anywhere from 3 minutes to 30 minutes. It is only when the physician will actually discuss the products and everything related to them along with disease states and patient welfare that you have really succeeded in gaining quality time. Quality calls are the ones that allow you to influence and change physician's prescribing habits. Dropping samples does not accomplish this goal. Dropping samples helps support current customers. It doesn't win future customers.

- **Showing Up!** Staying motivated and showing up for work every day when no one is standing over you is considered the biggest challenge that sales representatives face by many district managers. Even a mediocre pharmaceutical sales representative can do an acceptable job if she just shows up for work. Obviously, you can't get the job done if you aren't there. This job, in particular, requires a personal appearance. Burnout is one of the greatest obstacles that causes interference with a pharmaceutical sales representative's job.

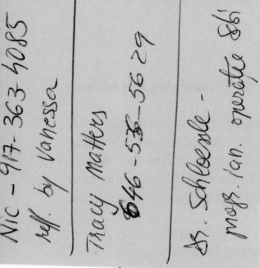

with a physician?

ons you will be able to ascertain the answer to this question. You icians has established for contacting him. Most physicians can be e their offices under certain circumstances. **Be sure to mention he new PhRMA Code rules and know what those rules are.** d time with physicians are:

etings
- Journal Club Meetings
- Golf course, etc.
- In-service Programs or "Lunch and Learn" programs
- Speaker Programs (Lunch or Dinner Provided)
- Lunch out for physician and colleague.
- Educational Programs for patients at the office
- Referral from his mentor or well-respected specialist
- Helping out with the physician's pet project as approved.
- Developing rapport with members of his staff
- Creating new ways to gain time with the physician

57. **To be a successful pharmaceutical sales representative you must differentiate yourself from the many other representatives in the field. Give me some examples of how you would do this.**

- **Always have something to say!** Some representatives make the mistake of just showing up and asking for a signature or showing the physician the same information over and over. This is boring for the physician. It doesn't help him and it makes the representatives look less than professional. Always offer good information that the physician will find useful in his practice.

- **Put the patient and physician first!** Don't ever allow yourself to be perceived as self-serving, only wanting to push your products. Your goal should be to help the patient receive better treatment and to make the physician's job easier.

- **Be a resource!** Be an eternal source of information. If you don't have the answer, get it! Difficult questions will arise during your conversations with physicians. For example, an extremely difficult question concerning how your product is absorbed, the enzymatic activity of your product and adverse reactions that could occur because of these properties could be asked by your physician. Maybe you know the answer. Maybe not. If you don't, your company's medical department will have experts to answer the question. Offer to place the physician in contact with the medical department immediately. Normally, you can pick up his phone, call the medical department and get an expert on the line immediately to answer the question. Now you are no longer "just a rep," you are a partner!

58. How pressured do you feel by the sales goals in your current position?

There's always pressure, but it's a good kind of pressure. You could always state that no one pushes you half as hard as you push yourself. You think sales goals are good as are goals in every area of your life. In order to stay on track and achieve to your full potential you must set goals as milestones of achievement to pursue.

59. The pharmaceutical industry has always been a product-focused industry selling their products through efficacy and safety. Over the last several years a new selling environment has emerged. Can you tell me what that selling environment is?

The new selling environment is one that focuses on education and product value. More emphasis on disease states, treatment programs, and being educational partners with the physicians has emerged. This does not mean that products are not presented and that efficacy and safety are not covered. They are. This information is combined with the new focus information that allows for better rapport and more customer focus. This selling environment allows you to partner with the physician. This is necessary in order to succeed in today's selling environment.

60. Let's say that I have hired you. Now I have given you a list of the physicians in your territory along with sales data covering their prescribing habits. Tell me how you would organize and prioritize your sales call schedule.

Respond like this:

- First of all, I would look at my physician's potential. That means that you would see who writes prescriptions for your type of product and who has large practices and therefore writes more prescriptions for your type of product.
- Next, I would see how many of the large potential physicians already write for my product. These physicians will be my "bread and butter" and will require maintenance and encouragement.
- Then, I would see which large potential writers are not writing my product. They would be major conversion targets.
- Following this, I would look at medium potential writers who write and who do not write for my product.
- I would go through the entire list of physicians this way and set goals based on writing habits and potential.
- Calls and call frequency would be based on the physician's potential to write and current prescribing habits. I would do this in order to maximize my sales results in the shortest period of time. This is working smart!

Have you heard about the 80/20 rule? That's what the previous dialogue has actually covered. Approximately 20% of your physicians will write 80% of your product prescriptions. You always maintain your base and up-sell your base. Then you focus on adding business by looking at physicians who have the greatest potential to help you.

61. Can you take criticism?

You must show that you do not take constructive criticism personally. You thrive on it! It is an opportunity to evaluate yourself and/or your performance. This can only help you improve your selling and your people skills. It's an opportunity to learn! Show that you can take constructive criticism without getting personally involved.

62. How do you feel about "paperwork?"

It is all right to say that it is not your favorite area of work, but that it is necessary. You must let them know that you realize that paperwork serves a useful purpose and must be completed on time as required. There must be some way of tracking sales, tracking sales performance and evaluating sales performance. If you like it, great!

63. What type of reports do you currently prepare as part of your job description?

Preparing concise, accurate, and insightful sales reports is important. New information must be passed on to your management immediately in order for the team to function well and surpass the competition. When everyone reports correctly, new trends, good and bad can be identified quickly and appropriate action can be taken. Areas of excellence and areas of deficiencies can be determined. In asking you what type of reports you prepare, they really want to know if you can write the type of report you will need to write as a representative.

64. Pharmaceutical sales representatives stay very busy. However, they must stay current on their product/medical knowledge. How do you think they find time to do this?

First of all, pharmaceutical companies offer continuing education classes/training to their representatives. The continuing education classes are mandatory. Some types of continuing education classes will create opportunities for upward mobility in the company. Some of the continuing education programs are geared to representatives who have shown an aptitude for a special area of influence within the pharmaceutical industry. Time is arranged for pharmaceutical sales representatives to improve their selling skills and product knowledge.

Second, improving your selling skills and product knowledge must be a personal objective as well. Time spent in the pursuit of improving your ability to perform is time well spent. Pharmaceutical companies have libraries that furnish materials to help you do this. Tapes and CDs are offered that contain selling and product information. Using these tapes and CDs while driving around in your territory and during "down time" helps you make the most of your time during the day.

Additionally, most pharmaceutical companies provide computers to all of their sales representatives for use in their territories and in their homes. Entering each sale call in your computer after you complete it allows better event recollection and prevents you from having to do this work in the evenings. If all call activity is entered during the day, you simply log on when you get home and transmit the day's work to your company. This leaves more time in the evening for family. Of course, this helps you balance company and family time.

65. Have you won any sales awards? If so, what awards?

It's all right to tell them what you have accomplished. Your statement will have more impact if you supply them with proof of your accomplishments.

66. Describe a sales situation where you turned a negative experience into a positive experience.

They want creative problem solvers because as a pharmaceutical sales representative you will have to do this on a regular basis. Cite a situation that started off badly with a customer, and then tell how you turned things around and "got the business." They want to know that you see these situations as "opportunities" and not as "problems."

67. Tell me about your greatest professional accomplishment.

This is the "what is your greatest achievement" question again. Tell them about the time that you made the fantastic sale, won the contest, created the best product in the company, etc. It's good to have some type of documentation to prove what you say.

68. Tell me about your greatest professional disappointment?

This is the "tell me about the time you failed to sell," "didn't get the promotion," etc. question. It doesn't matter what your answer is as much as it matters how you handled the situation. Tell them how you learned from your mistake or failure. Tell them what steps you took to "fix" the situation, and to be certain that your mistake or failure is never repeated. It's always great when you can state that you followed up and succeeded the next time.

69. What do you feel your chances of succeeding in the pharmaceutical industry are?

Excellent, of course! You must believe in yourself. Refer to the research you have done and the "field preceptorship(s)" that you have performed. Tell them you are very comfortable with the information that you have learned. You know that you possess the qualities that successful pharmaceutical sales representatives possess. Your business acumen is excellent. You are organized and efficient. Cite examples where you have sold tangible/intangible goods. Offer "proof sources" to confirm what you are telling the interviewer.

70. Do you currently work in a team-selling environment?

Pharmaceutical sales representatives must be team players! It starts at the district level and extends to the regional and national level. Everyone must play for the team in order for the team to win. If you are self-serving and divisive, you will take the team down. The district manager must be certain that you will place the good of the team above your own interests. Knowing that you are currently working in this type environment and that you are successful working in this type environment will assure him that you are a proven team player.

71. How do you feel about work guidelines, structured reports, etc.? Do you feel these are necessary or should you "wing" it?

Guidelines are necessary. There are legal considerations in the pharmaceutical sales industry. Let them know that you are aware that your company considers anything you say as a representative of the company to be a pharmaceutical company "claim." You realize the importance of making company approved claims and following guidelines.

72. How do you balance your career and family time?

In order to prevent burnout and to stay emotionally healthy and happy, you must be able to separate and balance career and family time. The district manager will look for proof from you that you currently do this and recognize that it is important. Additionally, those people who accomplish the balance have to be very well organized and efficient at time management. This is crucial to your success as a pharmaceutical sales representative. Just be sure that you emphasize your ability to balance family and work time.

73. Are you mobile? Are you willing to relocate?

If you are, this can be very beneficial to you. If you are not, now is the time to say so. If you are not mobile, that will not usually eliminate you as a possible employee. Most companies prefer to hire local people because of their community ties.

74. Do you feel strict rules of conduct are necessary?

Yes. Let them know that you are aware that you are representing the company, and will be seen as "the company" in the eyes of the physicians. Your reputation and the company's are tied together and must never be compromised.

75. Would you rather be "right" or "win?"

A major company very recently asked this question during an interview with one of our customers. This is a deliberately vague question designed to create discomfort and designed to see what your first response will be. **Your first response gives them insight into your "true" personality.** First of all, you should clarify the question, by restating the question to make sure that you understood the question. This is the same approach that you would use with a physician if you were unclear about the question. When you attempt to clarify the question, you are responding correctly. That is probably all you really need to do with this question. You could take it further and use this approach:

Sir/Madame, if you are asking whether I would always do the "right thing," then of course, I would. If you are asking if I always "have to be right," then NO, I don't. No one is "right" all the time. No one knows everything. We can always learn new useful information.

I would always try to "win" the business, because that's part of my job and obligation to my company. I would always try to "win" the business the "right" way by doing it ethically and morally. Pharmaceutical sales representatives have a tremendous responsibility. They must be honest about their products. If they are not, patients can be hurt or killed by misinformation. Pharmaceutical sales representatives must be honest with physicians, or they will lose their trust and that will be the end of the representative's career. That would damage the company's reputation as well and perhaps even place the pharmaceutical sales company in legal jeopardy.

At this point, the interviewer should be more than satisfied with your "true response."

76. You were just greeted by an irate physician who is having a very bad day? What course of action would you take?

First you listen and observe! You have to know what is happening to make a good decision. If the physician is just having a bad day in general and it does not relate to you, then should just show empathy and reschedule your appointment because you understand today is not a good day to talk with him. This will accomplish two things. First of all, you have shown that you are a considerate person and this will make you look good to the physician and his staff. The next time you show up at the office they will all remember your actions during your last visit and you will probably be allowed to see the physician and may get more time with him. Next, it's never a good idea to speak with someone who is so distracted that he can't give you his attention. How could you possibly sell him anything when he's in this frame of mind? You can't. Going back on a better day when he can focus on your message and really participate in a product discussion with you will give you good quality time with the physician. That's what it takes to change his opinion of your product and win his support.

77. How many "quality" total office calls per day can be completed?

Eight to ten quality office calls can be made. This is true because very often you can make "clinic" appointments that allow you to have good selling time with 4-12 physicians during a one to two hour time period. This helps to make up for those days when you do not have as much planned activity and you must make more "cold" calls. The 8-10 calls would be an average daily number and be certain that you state it that way.

78. Give me an example of your ability to learn technical information.

If you have a science degree, e.g. chemistry, you could have a copy of your college transcript available and you could point out (Use as a proof source!) how well you performed in your science course work, and therefore have proven that you can master technical information. Maybe you have mastered a technical course in some other discipline? Perhaps you have taken a continuing education healthcare course? Perhaps you have mastered an engineering course?

Perhaps you have learned technical information on your own and then used that information to help you perform better on your job? You will need to convince your interviewer that you are capable of learning technical scientific information.

79. You call on a physician with whom you have a scheduled appointment, but he is not in when you arrive, what is your course of action?

First of all, you must ask questions. Is the physician just going to be fifteen minutes late or will the physician be one to two hours late? If the physician will only be a few minutes late, you should certainly wait. If the physician is going to be one to two hours late, you should ask if you can leave and come back and see the physician at that time. If the physician's staff replies, "No he will be too busy with patients" then you should reschedule your appointment. Your goal is to get good quality time with this physician. It is better to reschedule your appointment than it is to get "seconds" for a sample signature. If you can't talk with the physician, then you have no real opportunity to "sell" the physician on anything. Your goal is to always try to get good quality time with the physician when he is open and receptive so that you can persuade him to write prescriptions for your products.

80. You've just made a "cold-call" on a physician's office and asked to speak with the physician. The receptionist/nurse states that the Doctor doesn't see representatives. What do you do?

This is the "How do you see a 'no see' physician question." There is nothing unusual about this situation or the response that the doctor doesn't see representatives. Pharmaceutical sales representatives face this obstacle every day. In reality, there is no such thing as a "no see" physician. That just means that he doesn't know and appreciate the value of the service that you can provide for him at this time. It is your job to find a way to enlighten him! First, you obviously need to see him to do this.

Remember, every other representative out there is trying to accomplish the same goal that you are attempting to accomplish. They're all trying to see this physician! Some sales representatives have already alienated the staff by making up ridiculous excuses to see the physician and may have tried even more unprofessional things, like waiting at his back door in order to catch him leaving and speak with him. That is an inexperienced sales representative's desperate attempt at a call and a fatal career mistake where this physician and his office staff are concerned.

Proceed as follows:

- Be very pleasant. Say you understand. Then ask if there are any special times when representatives are allowed to see the physician. Some "no see" physicians do see representatives when they have new products.
- Ask if the physician is a member of the local medical society and if he holds any office within it. You know he's probably a member, so you will get a yes. Mention that you support the activities of the local chapter and you want to make certain that the physician is aware that you can be counted on to help. You'd be surprised at the information that

you may be given at this point! He may be working on some project and may need your help that very day. I've actually had the receptionist get up and speak with the physician who called me in at that very moment to speak with him. Be prepared to deliver on your promise to help!

- All of the physicians will see hospital patients. Ask if he ever sees representatives at the hospital and if so, how do you set up an appointment to see him there. You may find that he sees representatives at hospital displays.
- Ask if the physician is a member of the Journal Club at the hospital. If so, state that you would like to offer support and would love to speak with him to discuss ways that you could support the group.
- Ask which specialist he refers to or if he is a specialist, ask for the names of some physicians who refer to him. Phrase this carefully.

By now you've got the idea! The physician has to participate in some type of continuing medical education program and he has to stay current on product information. You just have to ask smart questions and probe to find out how he accomplishes this. When you find out how he stays current on products, you will discover a way to speak with the "no see" physician. (See question 118 for more details.)

81. What do you think the differences are between a "sample drop" and a "sales call?"

"Sample drop" is just allowing the physician to sign for samples when he is too busy to speak with you or will not speak with you. A sales call occurs when you actually have time to discuss at least one feature and one benefit of your product and you have a real opportunity to advance the sale. Your goal as a representative would always be to attempt to gain time with the physician to have a real opportunity to influence his thinking about the product. Sometimes you do have to "sample drop." This may be the only way to get started with some physicians or maybe a good physician who usually sees you just doesn't have time that day. If you are understanding and allow the physician to sign for samples, then the physician will remember your consideration and talk with you the next time you call on him.

82. How do you determine what the physician's prescribing habits are?

You can be certain that your company already knows what the physician's prescribing habits are! They just want to know how you think you would find out what his habits are. You should respond with the following:

- First, I would listen to what the physician says. A successful representative always listens!
- Next, I would ask questions about his patient population and his favorite class of drugs to treat different disease states to find out about his preferences.
- I would call on pharmacists and other key medical personnel who may have insight into the physician's prescribing habits.

83. How do you develop rapport with a physician?

Developing rapport with a physician takes time and effort. First of all you must show up on a regular basis. Make your calls. Prove yourself as a valuable resource and partner. Show him that you value him as a person as well as a customer. Prove that you are trustworthy by being trust worthy. Prove that you are reliable by being reliable. Soon the physician will realize that you are someone who can be relied upon to give honest, useful, information and he can count on you to always be responsive to his needs.

84. Which is more important in a selling situation: the "opening" or the "close?" Explain why.

Handle this one carefully! The "correct" answer that they are looking for could be either the "opening" or the "close" or both. Stating that they are equally important and then giving an explanation about why they are equally important should be considered the best answer. Why? If you don't open well, you will not have the opportunity to close! However, a great "opener" is useless without an equally great "close." Both are equally important and must always be used in any sales presentation and I have attempted to explain the reasons why this is true in the information that follows:

First of all, **you must have a good "attention getting" opener or the physician will not listen to your presentation and give it any thought.** In order to have a successful sales call the physician must listen to what you are saying and then YOU must listen to what he has to say. You must then address his concerns or questions and use proof sources wherever necessary to address his concerns and answer his questions. If you do not open well, you will not have the opportunity to get through the sales presentation. If you do not open well, you will not have the opportunity to CLOSE.

Second, you have to CLOSE if you want the business. **If you want the business, you have to ask for it!** When you ask for a commitment and the physician gives you one, he feels obligated to follow through with the commitment. The physician is much more likely to follow through and write your product if he has stated that he would do so. Always close after you have earned the right to close. You should have adequately responded to any questions that may have arisen during your dialogue with the physician. When the physician gives signs that he has "bought in" to your sales message, then you close. These "signs" are "yes" nods of the head, verbal agreement or a statement from the physician about a patient who needs the drug and he wants samples, etc. Explain it as I have suggested attaching equal importance to the two and explaining why. I don't think you could possibly miss this one if you do this.

85. You are leaving samples for an office and notice that all your samples from a previous call have been "buried" by a competitor. What do you do?

Report the problem to the office manager or nurse, whoever is in charge of the sample closet. Just say something like, "Dr. Jones just signed for these samples because he thought he was totally out of samples. He wasn't! My samples have been covered by samples from another company. Can you please take a look at this?" Let the nurse/office manager see the situation! That person will realize what the other representative/company has done. Let them take it from there. They may ban the other representative from the office. They may also change the rules concerning where you place samples. Just be extremely nice and cooperative with the staff. Tell them that samples are very valuable and you are aware of this and you know that they are aware of this also. Tell them you have always appreciated the way they value the samples that they receive! No samples should be wasted because they are hidden. Also state that you want this office to always have your samples available for their patients. You always give them good service because they are very important to you, etc. This should provide the start of the solution to the problem and you will have represented yourself and your company in an excellent professional manner.

86. A sample shipment arrives at your home, but it is twice the regular amount of material. What do you do? Why?

Follow your company's policy regarding sample shipments. They always have established procedures. Very often there are legal reasons for the established procedures and the procedures are not just to keep the bookkeeping straight. There are established procedures for logging in sample shipments to your computer inventory. Your company will provide instructions for whom you should call, email, etc. about the double shipment. Additionally, you always keep your district manager in the loop. Copy him on all company correspondence or voice mail him. Why do you do this? You report directly to your district manager. It is your responsibility to keep him informed about your daily activity and about any problems that you may encounter. It's your job and responsibility to follow your company's guidelines regarding sample procurement and distribution.

87. While working in your territory, you meet a former colleague who wants to trade samples with you. How do you respond? Why?

NEVER! You can only legally leave samples with a licensed physician. You cannot give them to or trade them with anyone else. Your company will have strict rules regarding samples and you must follow them to the letter. Tell the person that you will follow the company's rules regarding samples just as you will follow the company's rules with everything else!

88. What do you feel you can offer the company? Rank in order of importance.

What do you bring to the table? Think about this! For example, you offer the company:

- Time (You must spend the time in the field selling in order to be successful. Your success makes the company successful.)
- Knowledge and selling skills
- Loyalty
- Dedication, Persistence, Enthusiasm (Whatever it takes to get the job done!)

- Creativity
- 110% effort.

You could also list all of these things and label each one as #1. They are all equally important!

89. Please circle the A.M. starting time and the P.M. quitting time you can regularly work for the company.

A.M. 8, 9, 10, 11
P.M. 12, 1, 2, 3, 4, 5, 6

You should start at 8:00AM and finish at 6:00PM. Even if you leave your fieldwork at 5:00PM, you will still have some paper work or computer work to finish. Sometimes you have to see physicians after 5:00PM. They just want to know that you will give 110% to your job.

90. What is your current salary?

Personally, I don't feel that what you make is any of their business, but they can and do ask for that information. Usually, they do this after they have decided that you are a serious candidate. They ask in order to find out what they should offer you as a starting salary. They will want to hire you for the least amount possible within the hiring range. Be aware of this because you want the highest starting salary that you can negotiate. You may attempt to get around the question initially by asking them a question in response.

Just state that pharmaceutical sales representatives have informed you that salary history is only an issue for those who are being offered a position. Then ask if they are offering you a position. If they are, what do they offer their best candidates because that is what YOU are, the best candidate. If they are not offering a position, that should end the salary history discussion. Just be careful about your tone of voice and body language. Do not appear resentful of the question. It is okay to appear excited about the possibility of being offered a position. Anyone would be excited about being offered a pharmaceutical sales position! If they still pursue this line of questioning, you will have to give a direct answer. Be certain that you state your "total" yearly compensation. For example, that would be salary plus bonuses, etc. rather than just salary. Answer truthfully, but don't sell yourself short! You can negotiate a higher starting salary if you already receive good compensation for your work.

91. The physician ,who is a big client, that you have just attempted to sell your product to has turned you down. What do you do?

Being turned down by a physician is an everyday experience. First of all, it is great that the physician is speaking with you honestly. You know where the physician stands. If the physician has stated the reason why he will not write your product, then the physician has actually simplified your job. Why? You now know what the physician's true objection is and you can deal with it! **This is a selling opportunity!** Those physicians who do not level with you about where they

105

stand are the greatest challenge! The best approach to use if the physician does not volunteer the reason he has turned you down is:

- Tell the physician that you appreciate his honesty. Never act defensive when the physician is giving you information.

- Tell the physician that you have tremendous respect for his opinion and you know that he has made the decision not to write your product for a good reason or reasons. Show empathy!

- Ask the physician to please share those reasons with you because you are very concerned about why he would not choose to write for your product. If anything is wrong you want to know it!

- When the physician shares the reason, you will find that there is usually some misunderstanding causing the physician not to write for your product. The physician may think that your product has side effects that it doesn't have or a much greater incidence of a side effect than it actually has. Very often competitors mislead the physician about other products in order to sell their own products. Don't criticize the competition though. Just show correct information. Do not resort to negative selling. It will just make YOU look bad! When the physician realizes that your competitor has misled him, the competitor will lose credibility and product sales! You do not need to point out what they have done. The physician will know what they have done!

- First, acknowledge the physician's concerns and repeat them to make sure you understood them correctly.

- Next, address the concerns. Tell the physician that you certainly understand why he would not write your product based on the information that he has provided. Then, tell the physician that there has been some "miscommunication" somewhere and state that it must be YOUR fault. Take the blame. It makes you look good. Then show him information that will calm his fears. Offer proof! If the physician thinks your product has a 15% incidence of dizziness and it actually has a 1.5% incidence of dizziness, show the physician the side effect profile from your product's prescribing information. The physician will realize that he has misunderstood or been misinformed by your competitors.

- After you have done this, ask if the physician still has questions or concerns.

- If the physician does not have questions or concerns, ask if he would now write prescriptions for your product based on the information you have shown him and complete the sell. If the physician still has concerns, you must address them and overcome any objections before you can ask for the business.

92. How would you persuade a physician to write scripts for your drug when he is writing the competition's and has stated profoundly that he's happy with their drug?

The very first rule of behavior here is…never criticize the physician's choice or decision! If you do, you will immediately alienate him and you will lose your opportunity to convert him. **This is a selling opportunity!** This isn't a problem. Try this:

- State that you know that he speaks from experience and you appreciate that. Ask him to share what he likes about the product because he obviously likes it.
- When he gives you the information that you've asked for you have what you need to make your case. Don't try to "unseat" your competitor or ask for ALL of the business at this point because that isn't going to work.
- You are sure to recognize one type of patient where your drug should work better. Tell the physician you understand and are not asking him to stop using a product that he is happy with and getting good results with. Tell him it is because he likes the features and benefits of the current product that you are very sure he will like what your product offers. Normally, you are competing with a product in the same class that offers very similar features and benefits.
- Ask if he will consider trying your product but only in this one type of patient because you believe that he will be very pleased with what your product offers. Then tell him what your product offers this particular patient. By asking for a small change rather than all of the business, you allow him to maintain his loyalty to the other product and representative while giving you the opportunity to get some of the business. Gain a commitment.
- After he tries your product and likes the results, he is much more likely to be persuaded to prescribe your product for additional patient types. This is how you gradually win him over and get the business.

93. Why should we select you to fill the position over a candidate with prior pharmaceutical sales experience?

Answer the question this way: Different pharmaceutical sales companies have different sales training programs. As you know, some training programs are superior to others. As an employee of your company, I will receive the best sales training. There will be no "bad habits" to overcome. I will be taught to sell **your** way. I am "new clay," and therefore pliable, ready to be molded by the excellent sales training department at (the company who is interviewing you). The selling style that other experienced sales representatives have learned may not be compatible at all with your company philosophy. This can create problems in the field with physicians and affect your company image in a negative fashion. That will not be a problem when you hire me.

After all, selling is just the ability to persuade others to do what you have asked them to do. Think of times and instances where you were very successful at persuading others to see things your way and then act upon this new insight. You will find that you have actually been "selling" most of your life. Some companies will not hire "experienced" sales representatives for the reason that I have listed above. They do not want to be faced with the problem of trying to change learned behavior that the company does not support.

94. Explain diversity and why the company needs to utilize diversity.

Diversity means: instance of being diverse, different and refers to variety and multiformity. Why does a company need diversity? This may be easier to understand if one compares stock market strategy. One is more likely to be successful and reduce the risk of failure (loss of money) if one diversifies. When one invests in several different stocks or mutual funds then the risks are spread out among all of the investments and the overall risks are reduced. The opportunity for rewards is actually greater also. Some stocks perform better than others. If one chooses several stocks that have the potential to succeed, then surely most will and maybe all will, increase in value. When the pharmaceutical sales company has a diversified product line, then they have more opportunities to succeed and the risk of failure is reduced. If one product (example: hypertension treatment) falls below projected revenue production, then another product (example: asthma treatment) may exceed expectations for sales. This provides a healthy mix of product lines and treatment modalities. Having a diverse group of pharmaceutical sales representatives with different cultural and ethnic backgrounds, along with different educational and work experience backgrounds provides a rich mixture of talent for the pharmaceutical company.

95. What is synergy?

Synergy means, "to work together." It refers to a combined action or force. When referring to drug synergy it refers to the combined or correlated action of two or more drugs. Two drugs working together are more effective than either drug working alone. Synergy is necessary in order for pharmaceutical sales companies to be successful and survive. It is also a necessary ingredient at the basic level of the sales organization. District sales teams must work together to reach their sales goals. Working with other sales representatives within the district, region, and nation allows the individual sales representative to contribute to the success of the entire sales organization as well as to his own sales territory. When everyone works together as a sales team the results are much more effective than they are when everyone works entirely independent of the other team members.

96. Tell me about a time when your honesty and integrity caused a problem for you and how did you deal with it?

Pharmaceutical companies would like to have honest people working for them and they will attempt to find out if you are one of those people who will literally "do anything" to make a sell. They can't afford to hire dishonest people who will compromise the company and the customers. Just think of a time when you were asked to do something wrong and you did the right thing anyway even though you paid the price for doing so. Perhaps everything turned out well for you in the end because you did the right thing? You need to give a specific example here.

97. Tell me about a time when you had to make a quick decision and what was its outcome?

Pharmaceutical sales representatives must be able to "think on their feet" and make quick decisions. They are expected to show good professional judgment. This question is designed to see whether you have that ability. Usually, they want to know how you handled a problem when you had to deal with it without assistance from your manager. You may have had to deal with an angry customer. You would have taken immediate action to calm the customer and dispel the anger. You would have immediately taken steps to correct the "problem" that was within your scope of responsibility while complying with company guidelines. You would then have presented this information to your supervisor as soon as possible. The outcome would have been that the problem was resolved satisfactorily for everyone.

98. Tell me about a time when you had to sell someone an idea?

This should be an easy question for you by now! Be prepared to tell them about how you had to "sell" someone on your idea. Selling means to get someone to "buy in" to your idea, accept it and then take the appropriate action because of it.

99. Tell me about a time when you were selected to be a leader and how did it turn out?

Can you lead by example? Can you influence other people? They are trying to determine whether you have the "right stuff" to be a pharmaceutical sales representative. Just think about a time when you lead some group. In this capacity, you should have delegated the work and you should have motivated the people in the group to work together and to do so efficiently and effectively. Do you have information that you can share about when you were appointed to head a project? Did you recruit others to work on the project? Perhaps you volunteered as camp counselor and you created activities for others and then motivated people to participate? What type of leadership role have you played?

100. How is your work performance currently evaluated?

They ask this question because they want to be able to measure your success. They want to know how you rank compared to your peers. This will help them decide if you are a top performer. Think this over and be prepared to explain how you are ranked.

101. Do you like change in the workplace?

You must be flexible to succeed as a pharmaceutical sales representative. Change occurs quickly within the pharmaceutical industry. When rules change, the selling environment changes also and you have to adapt. He wants to know if you are flexible and if you can adapt to change easily. Answer the question with a "yes." You like the constant challenge of change. You like learning new things. While change can be a negative, change associated with growth is normally positive.

102. You've been notified that you've been selected for a special week of training at corporate headquarters and you leave in one week? How do you handle your territory while you are gone?

First of all, this will be part of your normal routine. You will go to meetings and you will attend company-training classes on a regular basis. You will also take company sponsored trips. Who takes care of your territory while you're out of town? What do you do?

Keep your customers informed! Tell them you're going to be out of your territory for one to two weeks. Ask what you can do for them now so they do not experience any inconvenience because of your absence. Then let them know where they can go for help if they need it. Everyone has voice mail. Tell them that you will be available to them through voice mail even when you're gone. If they have a problem, you will help. That's just good business.

103. Does your current manager provide help and leadership to you in your current position?

You should make every effort to answer this question with a positive response, a "yes." Be certain that you think this over and mention all the positives that you can including such good management traits as listed:

- Constructive criticism
- Open-minded
- Fair treatment
- Good direction and support
- Motivating
- Comfortable work environment that promotes creative thinking and rewards results

Whatever you do, do not criticize your current manager. This will only make YOU look bad.

104. What have you done to enhance or further your sales skills knowledge?

List any sales experience you may have gained. Perhaps you may have taken a sales course? Perhaps you listen to sales tapes? Perhaps you have read books on selling. You can purchase items such as these. You can also take classes at your local university to help you with "marketing" and "sales." Tell them what you have done to increase your knowledge.

105. Why do you believe you are the right person for the job?

This is the same "why should we hire you" question again. You have to prove that you have the right stuff for this profession. You accomplish this by giving examples of where you have worked to achieve goals like a pharmaceutical representative. You have to prove your ability to sell, to learn and to adapt. Paint a word picture of yourself that will describe you as a "pharmaceutical sales representative" by personality, talent, and experience. Then frame your "picture" with proof.

106. **What skills do you have that make you qualified for a pharmaceutical sales position?**

Use the information that you have gathered from your "career comparison" document to help you answer this question. You should have an excellent list made already. Don't hesitate to use your "career comparison" document to "show and tell." In other words, use it as a "visual" and a "proof-source."

107. **Which job responsibility of the pharmaceutical sales representative do you believe you would enjoy the least?**

The best answer would be to state that you truly believe that you would enjoy all aspects of your job! If you can't truthfully say that, you could say that although you believe you would enjoy everything about the job, the paperwork (or something more insignificant) would probably be the least enjoyable. Why? Perhaps you would enjoy it less because you would not be "selling" at the time and this part of the job wouldn't be as exciting. Just state that you realize that it is "necessary" even if it is less enjoyable. Whatever you would enjoy "least" can't be a major part of the job.

108. **Compare the work experience you have to that of a pharmaceutical sales representative.**

Refer to your "career-comparison" document for guidance. Prepare your document as outlined in the guide with the different key pharmaceutical sales job responsibilities on the left and your matching job experience on the right. Use this document as your proof source.

109. **May we contact your current employer? Co-workers?**

Just say "No." Most people would have their current position placed in jeopardy if someone called to ask about their job status. The pharmaceutical companies know this and expect a "no" answer. This would be a good time, however, to offer a list of business and personal recommendations to the interviewer.

110. **Write a complete sentence describing: Penn State, Basketball, Rochester Institute of Technology, "Myself," and "Sales Person."**

This is a "word association" problem/question. Yes! This is an actual interview question from a recent customer's interview. Based on where you live in the country, you may receive a similar question. The best way to help you answer this question is to advise you to expect a similar question using local information from your area. Think about what the "highlights" are for your area in sports, institutions, etc. It does not matter what kind of word association that they may request of you. Just be certain that you make *positive* statements. Find something good to say. For the "Myself and Sales Person" part, just describe yourself and "Sales Person" with an identical sentence using what you have learned about pharmaceutical sales professionals. Every person/institution on the list should be tied together by a common factor. Think about your answer and how to write this for yourself as an individual. Write your answer down and rewrite it until you feel you have it written perfectly. Read it out loud. When the question comes up during an interview, you will be prepared!

111. **What is a "heart attack" and what are the factors that cause it? (Because some people outside the medical industry do not know what myocardial infarction is or may not be comfortable using medical terms, the question was designed to take that into consideration. It is not the interviewer's goal to embarrass anyone by using a medical term they may not know or fully understand.)**

This is another recent question from the field. Many companies sell cardiovascular (blood pressure, stroke, and heart) products so I have included this question and the next question to benefit those people who will interview with companies who sell these products. The companies will expect you to be familiar with their major areas of research and company product focus. Therefore, if the company sells cardiovascular drugs you should know what a "heart attack" or myocardial infarction is provided you have thoroughly researched the company and its products.

A "heart attack" or myocardial infarction refers to an obstruction of blood flow to the heart resulting in dying or dead tissue in the obstructed area. Heart tissue cell death occurs in the affected area of the heart.

112. **Explain the difference between a "heart attack" or myocardial infarction, and a "stroke?"**

A "heart attack" refers to an attack on the heart (obstruction of blood flow to the heart) whereas a "stroke" is a "brain attack (obstruction of blood flow to the brain)." During a "stroke" or "brain attack," blood flow to the brain is diminished or blocked and brain cell death occurs in the affected area of the brain.

113. **Are you mathematical? Are you analytical?**

When they ask if you are "mathematical" or "analytical" they are attempting to find out if you are "left-brained." A good pharmaceutical sales representative must have a balance between the left and right brain. Analytical people are usually very **organized and efficient**. You have to be organized and efficient in order to **work smart** as a pharmaceutical sales representative. You must also have some "right brain" characteristics as well. You must be **creative**! You have to be able to think on your feet when things don't go as planned. They want someone who is **versatile** and who handles change very well. When they ask questions like these, try to avoid a direct "yes" or "no" and use the key words in this paragraph to describe yourself.

114. **If a pharmaceutical sales company only sells "proprietary products" what does "proprietary products" refer to?**

"Proprietary products" simply means that they have produced and own the products that they promote. They are not licensees for the products. Licensees sell other companies products under contract.

115. What is "co-promotion" or "team selling" of products and explain why pharmaceutical sales companies "co-promote" products?

Co-promotion of products is very common. Sometimes two and even three sales forces will promote the same product. Each sales force may have different or even the same sales goals. You will be given a list of your targeted physicians and your sales "partners" in your territory will also be given a list. Your sales territory will overlap with your "partners" on some if not all of these targeted physicians. The reason they want several people calling on the same group of physicians is so that these physicians will hear the sales message more often. Research has shown that the more the physicians hear the message, the more likely the physicians are to remember it and to buy in if the message is a good one. Research has shown that pharmaceutical sales companies sell a much greater amount of product doing this. Just state that you think that "team selling" is a great idea for the reasons that I have listed above. That makes you knowledgeable and a "team player." Pharmaceutical sales companies want both of these qualities in a sales representative. You would almost certainly be asked to make an itinerary that would take the other representatives' itineraries into consideration so that you could each call on the physicians during different weeks. It doesn't work if everyone shows up on the same day or the same week at the same office. That would just make the physicians angry. You would also set up "in-services" or "lunch and learn" programs plus speaker programs and coordinate call schedules with your sales partners to set these or other special functions up for the physicians.

116. We are a start-up company. How would you compare us to one of the giant pharmaceutical sales companies? Why did you choose our company?

The "start-up" company is a very new or very small pharmaceutical sales company just getting started. They want to know whether you feel such a company would be a good place to work and stay or whether you would just use them as a "springboard" to get a year or two of experience and then leave them for a major company.

Sometimes "start-up" companies are perceived in a negative light, because they do not have an established reputation with the physicians. However, if the company has good products, experience with these products will quickly give the physicians a good impression of the new company. Usually, a start up company is a great place to start your pharmaceutical sales career. Why? First of all, it will be easier for you to get hired by them. You could work for a year or two and get pharmaceutical sales experience and then move on to a larger company easily if you have performed well if that is what you have decided to do. You definitely would not make this statement to the company, but this is an option for you. Second, the start-up companies very often pay better than the large companies. They do this to attract better people. They also usually offer better opportunities for growth and you can move up quickly and gain experience in a start-up company in a few years that you may not have the opportunity to gain in a large company during your entire career. Why? You have less competition for promotions within a small company.

117.   How do you see a "No See" Physician?

This question is one that pharmaceutical sales representatives must deal with every day in the field. While this seems an unfair question to ask during an interview, it is being asked so the following information is being supplied to help you answer it:

- First, you must start with this question. Is the physician a primary care physician (GP, general practitioner, FP, family practice or IM, internal medicine) or is the physician a specialist (CD, cardiologist, etc.)?

- One way to get to a physician who will not see you to meet with you, is to invite the physician to a speaker program with an interesting theme, nice dinner (moderate under new PhRMA Code rules) for the physician and a well known and respected speaker. If the person who is speaking thinks highly of your product and recommends it during his speech, your physician is very likely to start writing your product. When the physician does that, he will want samples and suddenly you will gain access to the physician through his office.

- Another way to get to a "no see" physician is to find out to whom the physician refers. By this I mean who does this primary care physician send his patients to when they need to see a specialist? Let's pretend that you also call on cardiologists and you know several who write your products and love them. When you find out to whom your "no see" primary care physician refers, then you can ask your specialist, cardiologist, to intervene for you if you have a good relationship with the specialist.

- You can reverse the situation above if you have a specialist that you can't see. Talk to the primary care physicians who write a large amount of your product and who also refer to the specialist. They can help to influence the specialist sometimes, although the situation is usually that stated above.

- You can go into the "no see" physician's office and find out if there are any special circumstances where the physician will agree to meet with a representative. Sometimes there are special situations such as new product launches and planning medical society meetings, etc. when the physician will meet with sales representatives.

- You can ask the office staff to please give the physician some important information that you believe he would like to see. This information would be important studies, etc. where your product is the "winner" over the competition. Be prepared to give the staff some type of promotional item or cookies, etc. to make it easier for them to cooperate with you. Sometimes, you will have to do this over and over and eventually you will win entrance to the physician.

- You can also go to the hospital department where the physician spends some time. For example, if you are trying to see a cardiologist, then you would be wise to develop good relationships with the people who work in the Cath Lab at the hospital where the cardiologist has admitting privileges. Set up an "in-service" and include breakfast or lunch for the group.

Show up with a plan. Present good information and something more...something that will benefit them. You must always present yourself as an asset and a resource if you are to win access to these people and gain their support. These people can help you see the "no see" physician.

The same situation would be true if you were trying to see a "geriatric" physician. You could ask the "no see" geriatric physician's staff if he doesn't see representatives because he is so busy at the nursing home. If they say "yes," then you could ask which nursing home. If he is the medical director or spends time in the nursing home, you may want to set up an in-service for the nurses there. It's the same line of thinking again.

• Find out if there is a Journal Club where the physician has admitting privileges. If the targeted physician is a member of the Journal Club, you're in luck! Get yourself invited to the Journal Club meeting. Just find out if someone you already know is in the club and then offer to provide educational materials, modest food, etc. in order to be allowed to attend. Remember that these meeting are for physicians! You are the outsider and you will have to pay your dues before you are truly accepted. Be patient! Do not interfere with the meeting. It will take a little time to befriend the physician in this setting. This is just one of the many areas where patience and persistence will reap major rewards!

• Find out what the physician's hobbies and interests are. There may be clues around his office. Does he play golf? Do you? Find out where he plays. The days of sponsoring his tournament are gone but you may be invited to play on his team. There are many ways to see "no see" physicians. You just have to be creative and do your homework if you want to see them.

118. How do you get past the gatekeeper to the physician?

Who is a "gatekeeper?" The gatekeeper is the person who allows you to see the physician. Sometimes, the gatekeeper is the receptionist. Sometimes, the gatekeeper is the nurse, the physician's spouse or office manager.

Regardless of who the gatekeeper is, this person is very important! You must develop and maintain a good relationship with this person. Always be courteous! Be considerate of her time. Treat this person with respect, just as you wish to be treated.

If the day is hectic and everyone in the office is in a terrible mood, then this is probably not a good day to see the physician. Be understanding. Say that you understand that this is not a good day and ask if you can come back at a later time or another day when everyone is not so busy. You will instantly make points with the gatekeeper! Because you have shown consideration, you will be shown consideration in return. When you go back to this office at the recommended time, you will be allowed to see the physician. Additionally, the physician is much more likely to give you more time because he is not so busy. The physician is also likely to be more receptive to your message because he is not as stressed out as he would be if the office were in a state of chaos. Just use common sense and your people skills to win friends in every office that you enter!

119.   What do you do when the physician tells you that your product is too expensive?

One of the most common objections you will hear in the field is this one! Cost is an objection that you will have to overcome almost on a daily basis. **Your goal is to change the physician's perception of the value of your product or lower the cost of your product.** Since you will not have the authority to lower the price of your product, you must change his perception of your product.

- First, acknowledge the physician's concern about the price.
- Second, gather some information about the physician's patients. Are most of his patients covered by prescription insurance? Are they Medicare/Medicaid patients? Are they "cash" patients?
- Offer "features and benefits" of your product based on the information that you know, and have been given, about the physician's patients and about your product. Prove that your product is "cost-effective" and a good value.
- Gain agreement and ask for the business.
- Remember, the physician must see the product as a good value regardless of the cost. Make it worth the price!

120.   What do you counter when a physician admits using your competitor's product with good results?

This is the same question as #92. It's just worded differently. The answer is the same:

The very first rule of behavior here is…never criticize the physician's choice or decision! If you do, you will immediately alienate him and you will lose your opportunity to convert him. That's what this is. It's a selling opportunity! Try this:

- State that you know that he speaks from experience and you appreciate that. Ask him to share what he likes about the product because he obviously likes it.
- When he gives you the information that you've asked for you have what you need to make your case. Don't try to "unseat" your competitor or ask for ALL of the business at this point because that isn't going to work.
- You are sure to recognize one type of patient where your drug should work better. Tell the physician you understand and are not asking him to stop using a product that he is happy with and getting good results with. Tell him it is because he likes the features and benefits of the current product that you are very sure he will like what your product offers. Normally, you are competing with a product in the same class that offers very similar features and benefits.
- Ask if he will consider trying your product but only in this one type of patient because you believe that he will be very pleased with what your product offers. Then tell him what your product offers this particular patient. By asking for a small change rather than

all of the business, you allow him to maintain his loyalty to the other product and representative while giving you the opportunity to get some of the business. Gain a commitment.

- After he tries your product and likes the results, he is much more likely to be persuaded to prescribe your product for additional patient types. This is how you gradually win him over and get the business.

121. **The physician won't commit to trying your product, nor will he tell you why. What do you do now?**

The noncommittal physician, the one who just sits and nods, or says "uh-huh" is by far the most difficult physician to sell. Why? First you must get the physician to speak with you in order to find out about his prescribing habits. After you get him to speak with you, it is possible to probe, ask smart questions, present features and benefits of your product and then ask for the business. With this physician, you have to find a way to get him to open up and start sharing his thoughts.

Some suggestions:

- Notice what types of patients are sitting in his waiting area. Does he see young patients, middle age patients, elderly patients or all of the above? If he is a GP or FP you should see patients of all ages. If he is an IM he may see all age groups but he may limit his practice. Let's assume that he only sees geriatric patients.
- We know that if he only sees geriatric patients he will most definitely treat hypertensive patients. For our purposes, your product will be one of the antihypertensive products.
- Mention that you noticed that many of his patients are elderly. Knowing that the elderly are especially prone to hypertension, you feel certain that Dr. A must treat many of his patients for this disease. "Is that a correct assumption Dr. A?" You should get a "yes" response out of this question.
- Now you would continue with, "Is there any particular treatment regimen that you favor for the treatment of your patients' hypertension considering their other health problems such as diabetes?" (You are setting the stage for introducing your product.) Now the physician should give more information because he should answer in the affirmative and then tell you which class of products he prefers. From there you would use your knowledge of the class to ask smart questions to get him to reveal what is important to him in choosing a particular treatment for these patients, and what if any, concerns he might have.
- Now you have reached a point where you can present your product and address his concerns.

122. **Your sales partner is going to the beach rather than to work. The physicians are angry and you are suffering because of this.**

First, you need to sit down and tactfully discuss the problem with your sales partner. Perhaps everything is not as it appears. Offer to help if there's a problem. You may be able to help your partner with a difficult situation and save her career. If the sales partner is not receptive to your offer for help or simply will not deal with the issue, you have no option but to speak with your district manager about the problem. The district manager will then be responsible for correcting the problem.

123. How do you sell products in a "managed care" setting?

Now this really is a tough question to ask anyone interviewing for an entry-level pharmaceutical sales question! First of all, don't assume that you are being asked how you would work as a managed care specialist. In reality, most pharmaceutical sales territory representatives do work in a "managed care" setting because managed care plays a prominent role in your physicians' practices. This is not the same situation as working as a Managed Care Specialist. Almost all of your physicians will accept either HMO or PPO patients. In a managed care setting how the physicians write prescriptions for these patients will be determined in large part by the HMO formulary rules.

First you have to know whether your physician practices within an HMO setting. There are different types of HMOs. Until you know what you're dealing with you can't form an effective plan of action. The best way to answer this question is:

- First, I would determine exactly what type of managed care situation I was dealing with.
- Next, I would become informed about the HMOs formulary and the process for formulary review.
- I would contact my company's managed care specialist for guidance with my district manager's approval.
- Together we would formulate an effective plan for selling products to the managed care physician.

124. Describe a "lunch and learn" or "in-service" program to me.

"Lunch and Learn" or "In-Service" programs are programs designed to help you gain more quality time with the physician. We know that everyone has to eat some time and most people will stop work long enough to eat lunch. The idea is to supply the food so that the physician doesn't have to leave the office. That is an immediate benefit for the physician. You can present your new product information while he enjoys his meal. This allows more time for solid product conversations and that gives you more opportunities to sell him on your product.

125. Often "in-service" programs are set up and worked by more than one pharmaceutical sales representative? How do you think this system works?

It is quite common for sales partners within a company and/or sales partners within two or three companies to get together to work "in-services" and "displays." Why? If you have three companies involved who promote the same product, that means you get to participate in three times as many "in-services" because every representative will have a budget for "in-services." For example, if you have the budget to fund three in-services, when you share the in-services with your partners you get to work nine in-services instead of three. You have tripled your number of opportunities to influence the physician's prescribing habits.

126. You have 12 physicians show up for your "in-service" program. How do you sell to a group of 12 physicians?

Having twelve physicians show up for an in-service is a pharmaceutical sales representative's dream come true! It does happen, but normally a few of the physicians within the group will get called out of the office. The selling process is the same with a small twist. You must include everyone as you speak. It's an excellent opportunity to have very in-depth conversations with your physicians about disease states, treatment options, and patient welfare. Usually, one or two of the physicians will immediately ally themselves with you. This is especially true if you have one dissenter (someone who doesn't like or use your product). Is this a bad situation? NO! It's great! The physicians who are backing you become stronger allies and normally influence the dissenter to change his mind about "not liking" your product. Getting all of these physicians together can result in a very enjoyable, lively, product discussion and information exchange.

127. Only one physician out of 12 made an appearance for your in-service and he says he only has time for a quick bite and a signature. How do you buy time with this physician?

Since you cannot change the number of physicians in attendance, make the most of your opportunity with the one who is there. Show no resentment of those who could not attend. If the one physician wants to sign and run, tell him you understand and ask if there's a better time to sit down and talk with him because you have some new information that you feel certain he's going to want to hear. He should either ask you to tell him about the information at that time or agree to set aside time for the discussion.

128. Where is the first place you would go when calling on physicians in a hospital environment?

I remember how crazy this location sounded to me the first time I was told where I should check in when calling on physicians in the hospital! Many hospitals will have pharmaceutical sales representatives check in at the Central Supply Room. Where is this located? It's usually in the basement of the hospital. There you will be issued a visitor's badge or name tag. You have to have a reason for being there. You must have an appointment in most instances in order to show up at the hospital. After you know your way around and you have made friends there, you may be able to visit some departments without going through the check-in process. Just know the rules and be aware of the consequences for rule violations.

129. **You are selected to work a "display" at a local medical convention along with pharmaceutical sales representatives from other companies. Tell me how you would plan for this day and how you would work after you got to the convention.**

There are different types of "displays," but this type is usually a major event. Pharmaceutical companies help fund the medical conventions that physicians attend. In return the pharmaceutical companies are allowed to set up their display units in a designated area. The physicians agree to go to the displays and speak with the pharmaceutical sales representatives during break times. A sufficient number of breaks are scheduled so that physicians can work their way around the display booths. In planning for your display you would:

- Organize your sales materials. Make sure you have a sufficient supply of the latest studies available for promoting your products. Have the latest visual aides available.
- Normally, special items, especially new items designed to help with product recognition are given to the physicians during these displays. You would make sure you had all of these items. These are normally items that the physician will use during working hours. Pens, note pads, paper clip holders, and prescription pads are popular gift items.
- Your display will have large colored panels displaying pictures of your products along with bullet-point features and benefits of the products.
- Your job is to set up your display in a good location where you will have good access to the physicians. To do this, you need to get there very early and find out where most of the speaker programs will be held.
- Next, you will set up your display in an organized and attractive manner.
- Then you will present your product to physicians who visit your display.
- Last of all, you will have a great opportunity to mix with the local representatives and gain more understanding of the industry as a whole as well as your individual competitors.

130. **"SELL ME SOMETHING!" How do you "sell" the district manager something, especially one of THEIR products?**

This is the **ultimate question** because you have to **PERFORM** to pass this one. The following information should win the position for you if you have practiced your selling technique and have made the necessary preparation.

My recommendations for this sales performance are:

- Collect pictures of the company's major products. There is no need to look at more than three products and you can probably get by with working on one product.

- **Example:** Select the major product of the company that you will be interviewing with, especially if it is #1 in sales for its class. Get pictures from magazines, the Internet, and medical journals (New England Journal of Medicine, JAMA, etc.) Make sure that these pictures are neat. Laminate them if possible. If not, at least place them in plastic sheet protectors. Use these pictures as your "visuals" for sales presentations. Show and tell!

- Read the information in the P.I. (prescribing information) that you find with the pictures. Pay close attention to the indication and the side effects as well as contraindications and warnings. You will need to know this information for "sales presentations." Make a copy of the entire piece of prescribing information. If you see something that looks very positive on this information, highlight it with a yellow marker. If they print some of their study results in the P.I. and it looks good, highlight it in yellow. You can point to these areas during your sales presentations. These highlighted P.I.s will be your "proof" sources. Don't highlight everything! Limit the highlighting to a few key words.

- Place the items you have collected in a binder, preferably one that has a clear insert on the front cover so that you can either create a visual to insert in the front cover, or so that you can insert a picture of their product in the cover. You should have dividers between each section of product information for each product. Be sure the sections are labeled and very neat.

- After you have done this for each product, look up information on the major competitive product for each of the company's products. Get pictures of the competitor's products and analyze the competitor's P.I. just as you did for the first product. (Example: If you choose ABC [pharmaceutical sales company] product A, then look up information on XYZ [competitive pharmaceutical sales company] product B as the competition.) You must present the company's product that you are interviewing with as superior to the competitor's product. You must compare two products in the same class. In other words, they must have the same indication and have the same basic mechanism of action. Pharmacists are great people to ask if you aren't sure which product competes with another!

EXAMPLE: COMPARE TWO ANTIHYPERTENSIVE PRODUCTS

Product A (Product A is made by the company you are interviewing with.) works longer (has a longer half-life) than **Product B** (competitor's product). It offers longer blood pressure control. Product A also lowers the blood pressure more points than does Product B on both systolic and diastolic blood pressure. Offering longer blood pressure control ensures that the patient has better blood pressure control coverage and no "unprotected" times during the day. Lowering the blood pressure more points and getting it within normal range means that the treatment is efficacious. This helps protect the patient from the ravages of uncontrolled elevated blood pressure and all the organ damage (heart, kidney, etc.) that comes with it. (Stating that Product A has a longer half-life is a "feature" of the product. Stating that Product A give better blood pressure control, no "unprotected times," lower blood pressure readings, and protection from the ravages of uncontrolled blood pressure are all "benefits" of Product A.)

You are helping to protect the patient from the devastation of stoke and maintaining their quality of life. Look at how often the patient has to take the drug. Is it once a day versus twice daily? Obviously, once a day is better. (Product A is dosed once a day and Product B is dosed twice daily.) The patient who is taking Product A is less likely to miss a dose. The more often a person has to take a medicine; the more likely that person is to forget a dose. (These are more benefits of Product A's longer half-life.) Be sure to check for agreement from the person that you present this information to during your presentation. (Example: "Wouldn't you agree…?" "Isn't that what you look for in an antihypertensive medication?" "Do these features match what you look for in an antihypertensive agent?")

After they agree, try a brief summary, starting with "We've agreed…" Restate the points that you have agreed upon.

At this point you attempt to close. **Ask for the business!** <u>**Always**</u> **ask for the business!** If he says "yes," I will prescribe this product. Say "wonderful," "great," "thanks," etc. to show you appreciate his commitment. Ask how many patient sample packs he thinks he will need over the next four weeks. This solidifies the sale.

- Create a "sample signature" pad. Just design something in Excel on your computer. Make it half the size of a regular sheet of paper or less. At the top, have a place for the physician's name, address, phone number, and DEA number. Next, have their different products listed down the left side of the paper with the different strengths of each product. Just do this for the major products that they are promoting now. The rep that you have networked with can show you what their sample signature document looks like and can help you with this. You will need to be able to write in how many samples you leave. At the bottom, you will have a place for him (the district manager/interviewer) to sign for his samples. At the end of your presentation after you have asked for the business and completed the sale, you will ask him (the district manager/interviewer) to sign for his samples. Thank him and tell him you will see him in a few weeks. Give him your "card" and ask him to call you if he needs more samples or anything at all prior to that time.

- **The interviewer should be very impressed with you and you should get the job!** Pharmaceutical companies can ask an endless number of unusual questions. Pharmaceutical company interviewers are constantly trying to create new and more difficult questions. They also hire consultants to produce these questions that are designed to give them true insight into your personality. They know that you are going to answer everything the way you think they will want you to in an interview. They will be trying to find out what the "real you" really thinks. Just remember what you have learned from this book and keep a cool head when they surprise you. **Think before you speak!** Not only are they interested in your answers; they are also interested in how you react to a stressful situation.

APPROPRIATE QUESTIONS THAT YOU MAY ASK THE INTERVIEWER:

1. How did this sales position become available? Is this a newly created position or was the position vacated? If the representative left, was this a transfer or promotion?

Use tact when asking these questions. Normally, the district manager will give you a sufficient explanation and you will have no need to ask whether the representative was transferred or promoted. If the representative was terminated, the reason doesn't have to be negative but it could be so you shouldn't ask that question. There are other ways to find out this information if you need it.

2. Ask about the company provided training programs.

The district manager will enjoy briefing you on the training programs. Pharmaceutical companies have some of the best sales training programs in the world!

3. What qualities or qualifications would the ideal candidate for this position possess?

This is a great question and if you have the opportunity to ask this early in the interview, you have the opportunity to find out what qualities/qualifications the *interviewer* considers most important in a pharmaceutical sales candidate.

4. Ask about the territory's geographic boundaries and major clients.

At this point you will probably be shown a map of the territory and given a brief description of the major hospitals and other major accounts in the territory.

5. How does this territory compare to other territories within the district in regard to sales and size?

In order to treat representatives fairly, pharmaceutical companies give representatives the same size territories based on the number of qualified targeted physicians. This is not the same thing as the geographic size of the territory. In that way everyone is on an even playing field and has the same opportunities for bonuses, commissions, and those wonderful trips! Finding out how well the territory is doing with sales gives you an excellent idea of how much potential it has for growth.

6. What are the territory's total sales?

Generally, most pharmaceutical territories are in the one million plus range.

7. What is the current territory rank?

You may already have been given the answer to this question when you asked about the comparison to other territories within the district, but if you weren't it's a good question to ask.

8. How is rank determined?

This is important. Rank will be determined by sales, but may also be determined by other factors. Sometimes Performance Management Reviews enter into the ranking and can affect the ranking either positively or negatively.

9. How are commissions/bonuses earned?

Every company will have a different plan so it is important to ask this information.

10. How many new products do you have in your pipeline and what is the time frame for launching the new products?

The fact that you would think to ask this question lets the district manager know that you are well informed and understand the importance of the pipeline.

11. Does the company co-promote products with other companies? If so, how are the territories laid out?

Sometimes there will be "mirror" representatives within the same company or with several different companies. How and when you make calls will be decided by management normally. You will be placed on a three to five week call rotation schedule to maximize the benefit of co-promotion.

12. Which physician specialty would I call on most often?

This is a good question. Knowing whether your focus will be on primary care physicians and or specialists will make a difference in your call planning and presentation.

13. How many sales forces does the company have? What are the names of the different sales forces? How does one move from one sales force to the other?

Normally, there will be several different sales forces. They are:

- Pharmaceutical Sales Representatives
- Territory Representatives
- Territory Managers
- Specialty Sales Representatives
- Hospital Sales Representatives
- Managed Care Representatives
- Pharmaceutical Sales Trainers
- District Managers
- Regional Directors
- National Sales Director

The first three positions are just different labels for the same position. All other listed positions represent different positions. Moving from one sales force to another usually involves a base pay increase and a promotion.

14. Will the company continue to research and develop products in the current areas of specialization or will the company be moving into new or different areas of specialization?

Another great question! You can immediately determine whether the company will experience new growth quickly. If they do start promoting different classes of products, that means they will need more sales representatives for new sales forces and more current representatives will be promoted.

15. Ask the district manager to describe his management style.

This is extremely important. Of course, if you've done your homework, you should already know this. You can see if his interpretation matches the representative's who works for him.

16. Ask the district manager to describe the average career path.

This information varies by company.

17. How is the sales representatives performance evaluated?

This evaluation varies by company but total sales are always a major factor.

18. How often are the sales representatives evaluated?

Expect to be evaluated every six months to a year.

19. What is the typical time interval associated with the career path of a pharmaceutical sales representative within this company?

This information also varies by company but you should receive good information that will tell you whether people move up quickly in the company.

20. Let him know that you want the position and ask for a commitment to speak with him again about it.

Good sales representatives always "ask for the business!" You're expected to ask for the job.

Summing Up The Interview Process:

Checklist of preparedness:

- Have you answered all the questions asked of you in this guide?
- Are you comfortable with the "Pharmaceutical Company Requirements" area?
- Have you properly researched the company that will interview you?
- Do you know the local company representative?
- Do you have several clean unfolded copies of your resume and cover letter in your briefcase/attaché?
- Did you list your *Field Preceptorship* on your resume close to the objective?
- Do you have all of your **"proof-sources"** which may be required of you during your interview?
- Do you understand **"features"** and **"benefits?"**
- Do you have several clean unfolded copies of your list of references?
- Have you spoken with all the people you have listed on your reference sheet?
- Have you given careful thought to how you will handle the most uncomfortable questions that you may be asked based on the interviewer's knowledge of you?
- Do you have a professional business suit to wear for your interview?
- Have you made plans to arrive for your interview early? Do you have a backup plan should that one not work?
- Plan on doing everything you can days in advance; get a good night's sleep before your interview.

What Happens When You Are Offered The Job?

Typically, the pharmaceutical sales company will send an official job offer to you. The district manager will ask to meet with you again so that he can offer the job to you. At that time, the company will have all the details of your employment spelled out. The base pay that is being offered will be listed. If you are not eligible to earn commissions for three-six months, this will also be covered in writing. The job offer will also list benefits such as a company car, insurance, 401k plan, company credit card, profit sharing and vacation time. Now is the time to negotiate for a higher base if you feel that the base salary being offered is not a sufficient starting base salary. Remember that all of your merit raises are based on a percentage of this starting base. You must use your own judgment concerning whether you should push for more money and risk losing the offer! The more you get up front, the better off you will be for all the years to come. Make sure that no misunderstandings have occurred at this time. Now would be the time to correct any misunderstandings.

If you are still interviewing with other companies, do not mention this, but keep your options open. If you know that you would really prefer another position and feel that you are close to getting it, negotiate with the current district manager and increase the time interval until the starting date. Don't stop the interview process with the other company if you feel that they offer something that you really want.

Continue to research and network if you are not convinced that you have made the best deal you can make. Other opportunities can and do arise. Other applicants who have accepted positions may decline at the last minute due to a better offer. The original position that you thought you had lost may be yours after all!

What Happens When You Are Not Offered The Job?

Don't be discouraged because you have been turned down for a pharmaceutical sales position. The "norm" is to be turned down by at least one pharmaceutical sales company before being offered a position. Some of the "problems" are just timing. In some instances you could have had the bad luck of competing with people who are exceptionally qualified for the position through education and pharmaceutical sales experience. In that situation you would lose. Fortunately, most people with excellent pharmaceutical sales records are staying with their present company and moving up so you don't have to compete with them.

The fact that you have gained an interview or more than one interview proves that you "stand out" as a candidate. Because you were selected to "ride with a rep," you impressed the person who interviewed you. It is from this point on that you need to carefully evaluate everything that you do. Was there anything that happened during your "ride with the rep" that could have caused the district manager to think that you would not be a good pharmaceutical sales representative? Ask the person you rode with for an honest evaluation. Chances are there wasn't, but if there was, you can correct the problem. Additionally, ask the district manager for feedback on why you didn't get the job. Ask if he has recommendations for you that could help you perform better in your next interviews because you know you want to be a pharmaceutical sales representative and you are willing to work and do whatever it takes to get into the industry.

Chapter

11

The Right Stuff!

Questions You Should Ask Yourself.

- Do I enjoy planning my own day and working alone?
- Am I a self-starter?
- Am I capable of working without direct supervision?
- Do I have good communication/interpersonal skills?
- Do I enjoy talking with people?
- Do I enjoy social gatherings?
- Am I a good negotiator?
- Am I fair and objective?
- Do I enjoy being part of a team?
- Am I organized?
- Do I have a burning desire to achieve?
- Am I good at problem solving?
- Am I very creative?
- Can I tolerate constructive criticism?
- Can I endure being watched while I give a sales presentation?
- Can I get up in front of a group of my peers and give a sales presentation?
- Do I learn from my mistakes?
- Am I willing to practice to perfect my performance?
- Do I enjoy getting out and performing different types of work?
- Can I tolerate not having a set agenda all the time?
- Can I work under pressure?
- Can I meet deadlines?

- Can I take rejection?
- If asked, can I place the needs of the team above my own?

Career or Job?

"Pharmaceutical sales" is a career. It's not just a job. It is a very lucrative career. The goals are high, but attainable, and the rewards are sweet! Before you enter the world of pharmaceutical sales, you should ask yourself whether you want a "job" or a "career." This career offers a constant opportunity to grow, to learn, and to achieve. A career offers the paycheck and the job satisfaction plus the personal and professional growth. A job offers a paycheck.

Your Personal POA.

What is your personal plan of action? You know that you want to enter the world of pharmaceutical sales. Where do you want to go from there? After you enter the world of pharmaceutical sales, you will find that there are different ways you can move with your career. You can move up into specialty sales positions, management, training, and marketing. After you are more familiar with the industry, you will be able to decide where you want to go.

Personality/Coping Style.

Based on the information that you've received, do you feel that you have the right personality for the job? Do you feel you have the right coping skills for this career? A career in pharmaceutical sales is very rewarding. It is also a very demanding career. Those people who are "well suited" for the position will find the career of their dreams. They will literally love this career!

The Right Attitude.

How objective are you?

Can you separate yourself from your current situation and look at it without emotion? In order to perform well at this sales position, you need to be able to do this. This is also something that a potential employer will attempt to determine about you. You have to show an ability to set aside "feelings" and personality conflicts in order to make a good logical judgment about any issue presented.

Can you tolerate positive criticism?

Can you tolerate having your district manager make suggestions about how you can improve your performance, or handling of a difficult situation? A potential employer will not miss an opportunity to determine whether you can handle this. You must be able to do this whenever your district manager works with you, at meetings, and in the field.

Can you take rejection?

Every day people will say "no" in one way or another to your sales efforts. Can you tolerate this? Can you hear the word "no" and take it in stride? Can you be objective and realize that a "no" just means that you haven't supplied the customer with enough information to say "yes?" A "No" almost always means that the customer doesn't realize what is being offered and you have to find out where the misunderstanding lies. Can you hear a "no" and not take it personally? You must be able to do this if you are to feel good about your job and yourself.

Can you recognize the needs of others?

Can you put aside your need to "sell" your product long enough to find out what your customer needs? Sometimes we get so caught up in "selling" and "presenting" our information that we completely ignore the customer. **Good listening skills are just as important, if not more important, than good presentation skills.** Once again, your future employer will definitely be watching to see if you have good listening skills. They will want to know if you are empathetic.

Can you read body language?

Can you tell, just by looking, whether your customer is accepting your information or whether you are being ineffective? **"Always remember what you came for…" and pay attention to your customer's reaction.** Does the customer appear to be buying what you are selling? This is a very critical area in the world of pharmaceutical sales. Many people do not feel comfortable discussing areas of confusion or disagreement. Many physicians do not want to appear "ignorant" or "uninformed." You must be able to read body language and then have the ability to place people at ease. This is a necessary skill regardless of the type selling in which you are engaged. We will cover this more later, but **getting through your interview will definitely depend on your ability to read your interviewer's body language!**

Chapter 12

Purpose And Responsibility

Promote The Company's Product.

Your primary function as a pharmaceutical sales representative is to "sell" your company's products to physicians. To "sell" the product doesn't literally mean that the physicians will pay a purchase price for your product. When the physician is sold on your product, the physician will write prescriptions for your product. When the patient takes the prescription to the pharmacy the "sale" is complete. Different companies have different methods of tracking "sales." Different companies also have different methods of paying bonuses based on your product sales increase. Your employer will explain their method to you after you are hired.

Promote The Company's Image.

Always remember that "you are the company" to the physicians and the rest of the medical community. You owe it to your employer to present a professional appearance. Your conduct must always be above reproach. Remember, as a pharmaceutical sales representative you are a very influential professional business leader. Physicians and other highly educated members of the medical community will look to you for information, advice, and at times, leadership. Other members of the pharmaceutical community will also be affected by the impression you make.

Adhere To Company Policy.

Your employer has rules for a reason and many of them are legal ones. When you are given information, respect the instructions given with that information. Your responsibility as a pharmaceutical representative is a serious one. **What you say and do affects the lives of patients.** Your position is an important one. Treat it that way.

Loyalty To Your Company And The Industry.

There are different ways of showing loyalty to your company and the industry. Keeping confidential company information confidential is certainly a major one. Not only is this the right thing to do, but it is also the smart thing to do. Once again, repeating confidential information can have legal ramifications. Even if that isn't the case, repeating confidential information causes you to "look bad" and causes you to lose the respect of your colleagues and other people in the industry. **If you ever lose the respect of your customers, you may as well quit and pursue a different career**. Trust in this profession is of the utmost importance. The physician must be able to trust that the information you give to him is absolutely correct. Without trust, all is lost.

Another important area of loyalty is to the pharmaceutical representative profession. In order to perform well at this job, it is so important that all representatives uphold the high standards expected of everyone in this field. Any negative behavior will reflect badly upon every other representative. Remember that your actions never affect only you. Someone else will suffer also. On the other hand, if you uphold the high standards and even exceed them, then you bring honor to the profession. I am sure that everyone would choose to bring honor. It would only be through ignorance that a misdeed would be done.

Chapter 13

Career Path And Perks

ADVANCEMENT

- **Management.**

  Not only will you start at a very high level of income compared to most of the job industry, but you will also have wonderful opportunities for professional growth. After only a few years, it is possible to move into management if that is your goal. All companies have different time intervals for advancement, and different standards for advancement though both would be similar from one company to the next. In general, you can move into management in five years. Once you move into management, you can expect to earn a six-figure income, plus even more benefits and perks. Not bad for approximately five years of dedication and hard work!

- **Sales.**

  There are different types of sales positions. There are territory sales positions, special area sales positions, sales management positions and sales training positions. **Sales Training and development** is an area that appears to be a growing one within the pharmaceutical industry. Most companies have their own training departments dedicated to training their sales representatives for fieldwork. If you know that you enjoy teaching and you are a creative person, then this may be exactly where you would like to be. There are positions at the regional and national level in most companies. **Only the brightest and the best are allowed into the training departments because they are responsible for training a company's entire sales force.**

A listing of the available sales positions follows:

1. **Pharmaceutical Sales Representative, Territory Sales Representative** and **Territory Manager positions** are usually known as entry-level sales positions.

2. **Medical Specialist** or **Hospital Specialist** is the next level in sales positions.

3. **Specialty Sales Representative.** Medical specialists and specialty representatives are experienced sales representatives who excel at selling. They are "top-performers." With these promotions, you could expect to receive a substantial raise. Being mobile will also help you here. Some companies are more concerned than are others about your willingness to move up in the company. Others will not mind if you do not want to move up in the company. They know that they need a good solid base of territory representatives to keep the sales momentum going.

4. **Medical Science Liaison or Scientific Manager** requires a master's degree or a doctorate. These are pharmaceutical product/disease-state experts who meet with physicians to answer technical questions about products and disease-states. The advanced degree is necessary in order to have credibility with the medical community.

5. **Senior Pharmaceutical Sales Representative** normally requires a minimum of five years of successful pharmaceutical selling experience. Most companies require that the Senior Representative candidate be a top 25% performer for at least 75% of the time spent in the field.

6. **Pharmaceutical Field Sales Trainer** requires exceptional selling skills and years of top sales performance. Additional evidence of a gift for teaching is required.

7. **Regional Sales Trainer** is the next in-line promotion for the Field Sales Trainer. More management responsibilities are added.

8. **National Sales Trainer** is the top level promotion for trainers and is primarily a management position.

9. **National Account Manager** requires extensive contract experience and a confirmed solid knowledge of the pharmaceutical industry.

10. **Managed Care Manager** requires extensive sales and management experience and extraordinary negotiating skills.

11. **Government Affairs Manager** requires extensive sales and management experience and extraordinary negotiating skills.

12. **District Sales Manager** requires years of exceptional selling and management experience.

13. **Regional Sales Director** is the next in-line promotion level for the District Manager. There are very few Regional Sales Director positions available within any company. In order to be considered for a

promotion to Regional Director, a District Manager must rank consistently at the top of the District Managers' ranking system.

14. **National Sales Director** is the final in-line promotion level for Regional Sales Directors and this person has to be a master at EVERYTHING regarding sales, management and negotiation!

Awards

- **Trips.**

Can you imagine having someone pay for you and your "significant other" to take an all-expense paid wonderful paradise vacation? If you make the cut, you won't have to imagine this. In every company, the sales leaders are recognized and rewarded and this is one of the rewards! These top sales awards are given to the top five percent or so of the sales force. These people are recognized as President's Club or President's Circle winners. In addition to the wonderful vacation trip, there are dinners and presentations of company rings, etc. to honor the top performers. It is a goal well worth pursuing!

- **Monetary rewards.**

Of course, we all want more money! That's why we like the sales industry. Part of the reward for a job well done, is additional money. This may be earned as higher than normal bonuses, or additional cash rewards. In addition to the big money makers such as President's Club Winner, there are smaller rewards. There are contests that pay money. Many companies reward sales representatives for good selling ideas. **They know you want the money…most companies are ready to show it to you!** There are gifts and gift certificates. The perks' list continues!

- **Recognition.**

In addition to monetary rewards there is the satisfaction of recognition. Sales winners are recognized and rewarded at the district, regional, and national level. Top sales people are extremely valued by their companies. Surpassing sales goals and capturing top honors is a great way to get to know the people within your company who have the power to advance your career.

Benefits.

- **Company Car.**

How many employers value their employees enough to supply them with a brand new company car when they're hired? Not many, but this is one of the benefits of being a pharmaceutical sales representative! Not only will you get a new car when you're hired, but you will be allowed to order a new car whenever you get 45,000-50,000 miles on your "old" car. You are allowed full personal use of the car as well. That's right! You can use your car as your personal car. So what do you have here? You always have a new/almost new full-size car to drive for FREE. The company also pays for the insurance, and they either supply you with a gas card or reimburse you for the gas! You only pay for the personal miles you place on the car.

- **401k.**

Everyone is concerned about retirement, as they should be. Pharmaceutical companies really look after their employees in this area. Not only will you have the usual retirement plan, you will also have a 401k. With some companies you can participate immediately, and with others you may have to wait one year to start participating in the program. After you become eligible, you can place 1-15% of your earnings into the 401k plan. The pharmaceutical company will also match 3-7% of your investment. You're already making money! Sometime after one year (this varies) you become partially vested. Vesting means all the money in your account, including what your employer has contributed, belongs to you. Most plans will offer full vesting between three and six years. That means that you are entitled to all of your vested money should you decide to leave the company. **This is a fantastic way to save and if you start as soon as you're eligible, you have the potential to retire as a MILLION-AIRE!**

- **Profit Sharing.**

Simply put, this is an additional bonus that is paid out to employees when the company exceeds its monetary goal for sales. Some companies pay their employees 2-16% of their base salary based upon the company's performance and upon the individual or district's performance.

- **Insurance.**

Pharmaceutical companies offer some of the best health, and dental insurance available. Most offer a choice in plans…one that will suit your family's needs perfectly. Your contribution will be minimal. The company pays most of the cost. You also have excellent life insurance and disability insurance.

- **Retirement.**

In addition to your 401k, you will usually have a retirement plan. It just keeps getting better and better! This works like most retirement plans. You have to work a number of years and be a certain age to retire. You have the option of retiring at different levels in the plan. The earlier you retire the less money you will receive each month. This is true everywhere.

- **Other benefits.**

  Other benefits that may be of interest especially to those who have young families, is the dependent care benefit. There are also educational cost reimbursement benefits. Having someone else pay for the cost of your advanced degree is always a great benefit!

Contract Sales Organizations

Contract Sales Organizations or Contract Sales Companies supply pharmaceutical companies with part-time and temporary pharmaceutical sales representatives. These representatives are sometimes referred to as "flex-reps." Usually, they are given a mileage allowance because they must use their own personal cars for work. They may be paid a salary or given a set amount of money per physician signature. They are normally required to see 20-30 physicians per week depending upon whether the position is considered full or part-time.

This can be a good opportunity for gaining experience in the pharmaceutical sales field. If you have been unable to secure a permanent position with a pharmaceutical sales company, this is another option that could lead to permanent employment in the pharmaceutical sales field.

Contract Sales Organizations have experienced considerable growth over the past five years as the pharmaceutical companies utilize them more often. More and more often they are called upon to supply experienced pharmaceutical sales representatives for pharmaceutical company product launches and expansions. Sometimes the pharmaceutical companies just need a temporary boost in their sales force to push enough products to make goal so they utilize the CSOs sales force to help them do this. For this reason, permanent pharmaceutical sales positions also exist within the Contract Sales Organizations. You may find that you enjoy a constantly changing work environment and decide to work permanently with the Contract Sales Organization.

I have listed below the major contract sales companies:

Innovex, Inc.
Waterview Corporate Centre
10 Waterview Boulevard
Parsippany, NJ 07054
Phone: (973) 257-4500
FAX: (973) 257-4561
Web: innovexglobal.com
Direct Career Site Link: quintiles.com/careers/find_a_job/

Pro-Pharma
24 Queen Street East, Suite 900
Brampton, Ontario L6V 1A3
Canada
Phone: (905) 459-9728
Fax: (905) 459-9894
Web: pro-pharma.com

McKesson Pharmaceutical Partners
101 College Road East
Princeton, NJ 08540
609/919-3900
609/919-3931
Web: mckhboc-ppg.com

Nelson Professional Sales
41 Madison Avenue
New York, NY 10010
Phone: 212/684-9400
Fax: 212/684-3478
Web: nelsonprofessionalsales.com

Dendrite International, Inc.
1200 Mt. Kemble Avenue
Morristown, NJ 07960
Phone: 973/425-1200
FAX: 973/425-2100
Web Site: dendrite.com

Professional Detailing Incorporated (PDI)
10 Mountain View Road, Suite C200
Upper Saddle River, NJ 07458
Phone: 800/242-7494
Phone: 800/698-7491 (to apply)
Fax: 201/258-8400
Web: pdi-inc.com

Conclusion

Now you have completed that first most critical step forward! You have prepared yourself for a career in the pharmaceutical sales industry. You now have an advantage over most of your competition for the highly prized pharmaceutical sales position!

When I started my quest for a pharmaceutical sales position, I did not have the advantage of a "how to" guide. It took two years of trying, preparing, and learning what I needed to do to break into the pharmaceutical sales field. My father wasn't a physician or a pharmacist. I did not have an "inside track." The majority of people seeking pharmaceutical sales positions will find themselves in that same position. While those people with the advantage of an "inside track" are fortunate and may gain an interview without having to work as hard to get it, everyone still has to make it through all the interviews. This places everyone on an even playing field. In order to succeed at gaining a position as a pharmaceutical sales representative, one must be completely prepared. **The *"Insider's Guide to the World of Pharmaceutical Sales"* gives you the advantage!**

I wish you the very best of luck in your quest for a pharmaceutical sales position!

Sincerely,

Jane Williams
Author
Insider's Guide to the World of Pharmaceutical Sales

Appendix A
Pharmaceutical Company Profiles

On the following pages, you will find profiles of some of the top pharmaceutical sales companies in the United States, and in the world. A few companies may have been omitted. In some instances there have been mergers. Remember, there are constant changes within the pharmaceutical industry. **For the very latest information, you will have to research these companies on the Internet because changes take place daily.** There is a tremendous amount of information about the pharmaceutical companies available to you on the Internet. The lists in Appendix A should serve as an excellent starting point for your research.

I have researched some of the major companies for you and provided you with company profiles that include product and sales data. The pharmaceutical company profiles serve as examples of the information you should look for when you research pharmaceutical companies. These profiles will prove very useful to you when you gain an interview with one of these companies. **You should always research any company before interviewing with them!** You have no need to research all of them.

Following Appendix A is Appendix B which lists three hundred (300) pharmaceutical companies including web site addresses. **You should visit the web site of any pharmaceutical company that you want to research to find the latest information!** The fact that these pharmaceutical companies have not been researched for you does not indicate that they are inferior companies in any way. It simply is not practical to research every company.

3 M Pharmaceuticals

3M Center
Bldg.273–3W–01
St. Paul, MN 55144–1000
Phone: 651–733–1000
Web: 3m.com/pharma

Highlights

- Executive Vice President: Charles Reich
- Annual Revenue: $16.0 billion ($3.4billion-pharma)
- R&D 2002: $1.1 billion
- Sales Force Size: 1200
- Number of employees: 68,774 worldwide
- Operating in countries worldwide: 60
- Effective January 1, 2003 they reorganized into seven major businesses.
- Celebrated 100th anniversary in 2002.
- 3M acquired Riker Laboratories in 1970.
- Manufacturing operations with 32 labs.
- There are more than 40 business units in the parent company.
- They have formed an alliance with Berlex Labs to sell Women's Health Products.
- April 1, 2002 IVAX and 3M agreed to co-market QVAR inhalation aerosol.
- 3M has 501 U.S. patents awarded.
- Product development is based on (IRM) Immune Response Modifier Technology.
- 3M is collaborating with Eli Lilly on Resiquimod for Herpes.
- More than one-half total sales comes from outside the United States.

Major Products & Therapeutic Areas

Anti-Inflammatory	Musculoskeletal	Immune Response	Cardiovascular
Disalcid: Arthritis	Norflex: pain	Aldara Cream: HPV	Minitran: angina pectoris
	Norgesic Forte: pain		
			Tambocor

Women's Health	Respiratory	Specialty	Specialty
MetroGel-Vaginal	Maxair Autohaler: asthma	Urex	Urex
	Maxair Inhaler: asthma	Calcium Disodium	
	Theolair: asthma/COPD	Versenate: lead poisoning	
	QVar inhaler: asthma		

Pipeline Products

Antiviral	Oncology	Respiratory/Allergy	Specialty
	IRMs Aldara: extended indications		

Abbott Laboratories Ltd.

100 Abbott Park Road
Abbott Park, IL 60064-6400
Phone: 847-937-6100
Fax: 847-937-1511
Web: abbott.com

Highlights

- Chairman/CEO: Miles D. White
- Annual Revenue: $17.7 billion
- R&D 2002: $1 billion
- Sales Force Size: 3200
- Number of employees: 70,000 worldwide
- Operating in countries worldwide: 130
- Ranks #48 out of top 500 American companies for by Forbes Magazine.
- Top 10 Best Places for Working Mother magazine.
- October 9, 2002 announced plans to restructure in 4th quarter reducing work force by 2000.

- Acquired cardiovascular stent business segmentof Biocompatibles International plc.
- $20 million global HIV program in 2002.
- Co-promotes products with Triangle Pharmaceuticals and Boehringer Ingelheim.
- Abbott and Takeda Chemicals formed TAP Pharmaceutical Products as a joint venture.
- Acquired Vysis, December 2001.
- Have more than 5,000 scientists in R&D.
- Alliance with MedImmune to market Synagis.
- Agreement with MedNova, Ltd. and Rubicon Medical, Inc. to expand presence in cardiology and radiology markets.
- Alliance with Millennium in March 2001.

Major Products & Therapeutic Areas

AIDS/ Anti-Virals	Anti-Infectives	Metabolic	Neuroscience	Cardiovascular	Respiratory
Synagis: RSV	Biaxin	Tricor: cholesterol and triglyceride	Depakote: seizures; migraines; mania and epilepsy.	Isoptin/Mavik: hypertension	Xopenex: bronchospasm; pediatric ind.
Norvir: HIV	Biaxin XL				
Kaletra: HIV	Erythromycin	Meridia: obesity		Rythmol: antiarrhythmic	Zyflo: asthma
	Clarithromycin	Synthroid			
	Omnicef-peds		Precedex: sedative	Abbokinase: pul embolism	

Oncology	Urology/ Gastrointestinal	Anti-Inflammatory	Pain Management	Nutritional Supplements	Specialty
Lupron: prostate cancer Paclitaxel: cancer	Flomax: BPH	Humira: mod. to severe RA- adults	Depacote/ER: migraine pain	Advera: HIV/ AIDS	Survanta: neonatal RDS
	Hytrin: BPH		Mobic: rhematoid and osteoarthritis	Ensure	PSA test: prostate cancer
	Uprima: ED			Ensure Light	
Zemplar: renal					
Meloxicam: RA/ OA PathVysion	Prevacid: acid reduction		Dilaudid Vicoprofen Ultane: inhal.	Vi-Daylin	Gengraf: prevent organ rejection

Pipeline Products

Oncology	Respiratory	Cardiology	Pain Management	Anti-Infectives	Metabolic
Atrasentan	Xopenex	Simdax	D2E7: rheumatoid arthritis	ABT:773	Armada
ABT: 627					TriCor

Alcon Laboratories Inc.

P.O. Box 6600
Fort Worth, TX 76115
Phone: 817-293-0450
Web: alconlabs.com

Highlights

- President/CEO: Tim Sear
- Annual Revenue: $3 billion
- R&D 2003: $220 million
- Sales Force Size: 300
- Number of employees: 10,000 worldwide
- Operating in countries worldwide: 100
- Nestle, S.A. is the parent company.
- Started as a small pharmacy opened by Robert D. Alexander and William C. Conner in Ft. Worth Texas in 1945.
- Acquired Laboratories CUSI in 1995.

- Launched AcrylSof intraocular lens, the first acrylic soft foldable lens for small-incision cataract surgery. This lens became a $100 million dollar product in its first year of promotion.
- 2003- One of Fortune's "100 Best Companies to Work For" List for five consecutive years.
- Have 1,000 scientists working in R&D.
- Alcon has a voluntary turn over rate of only 5%.

Major Products & Therapeutic Areas

Glaucoma	Anti-Infectives	Anti-Inflammatory	Anti-Allergy	Ophthalmic Solutions
Travaton	Ciloxan	TobraDex	Pantanol	Emadine S. Sol.
Betopic S	TobraDex	Vexol: steroid	Alomide	Opti-Free Express/ Enzymatic Cleaner
Lopidine/Iopidine	Cipro HC Otic	Ciloxan	Emadine	
Azopt				Opti-Free Rinsing, Disinfecting and Storage Solution
Timopticxe				

Intraocular Lens	Comeal Topographer	Surgical Device/ Solutions	Phacoemulsification system	Specialty
AcrySof: used for small incision surgery	EyeMap: EH290	Accurus 200, 300, 400 and 600: delicate procedures in the back of the eye	Series 20000 Legacy	SupraClens Lens Cleaner
				Clerz Plus
Alcon Intraocular Lens (IOLs)		Viscoat		Lens Drop
		ProVisc Duovisc Sys.		

Pipeline Products

Macular Degneration	Anti-Infective	Anti-Inflammatory	Glaucoma	Anti-Allergy
Optrin	Paclitaxel Polymeric	New class of steroids	Topical prostanoids	

Amgen Incorporated

One Amgen Center Drive
Thousand Oaks, CA 91320
Phone: 805-447-1000
Web: amgen.com

Highlights

- Chairman/CEO: Kevin Sharer
- Annual Revenue: $5.5 billion
- R&D 2002: $1116.6 million
- Sales Force Size: 300
- Number of employees: 10,118 worldwide
- Operating in countries worldwide: 35
- World's largest biotechnology company.
- Amgen Award for Science Teaching Excellence announced January 14, 2002.
- Co-markets with Yamanouchi Pharmaceutical.
- Ranks #2 on Barron's List-best investor performance.
- Acquired Kinetrix Pharmaceuticals in 2000.
- Amgen has more than 10 products in develop ment.
- October 18, 2002 Amgen won a $150 million judgement against Johnson & Johnson for promoting Procrit into Amgen's reserved dialysis market.
- Amgen joined Wyeth October 17, 2002 to initiate a clinical trial evaluating a (TNF) Tumor Necrosis Factor inhibitor, Embrel, on (RA) Rheumatoid Arthritis patients in the United States.
- Acquired Immunex in July 2002.
- Expects sales to double in 2003.

Major Products & Therapeutic Areas

Hematology	Anti-Infectives	Anti-Viral	Bone & Inflammation
Aranesp: anemia associated with chronic renal failure including patients on dialysis and chemotherapy associated anemia	Neupogen: prevents infection in cancer patients undergoing certain types of chemotherapy and bone marrow transplants. It's also used for chronic neutropenia and to support acute myeloid leukemia patients.	Inferon: treatment of Hepatitis C	Kineret: biologic response modifier for reduction of symptoms of RA.
Epogen: anemia associated with chronic renal failure			

Hematology	Oncology	Oncology	Bone & Inflammation
Neulasta: single dose per chemotherapy cycle; decreases the incidence of infection	Novantrone: AML; MS; HRPC- Hormone Refractory Prostate Cancer	Thioplex: cancer	Enbrel: psoriatic/RA

Pipeline Products

Oncology/ Hematopoietic Factors	Oncology/ Hematopoietic Factors	Neurobiology/ Endocrinology	Specialty/Nephrology
rHU-KGF: aplastic anemia	Stemgen: bone matastases	LEPTIN	Osteoprotegerin: RA
Epraterzumah: non-Hodgkins	Calcimimetics: secondary hyperparathyroidism	Cinacalcet HCL-hyper parathyroidism	PEG-STNF-R1: RA
		GDNF: Parkinson's	Palifermin: mucositis

AstraZeneca

1800 Concord Pike
P.O. Box 15437
Wilmington, DE 19850-5437
Phone: 302-886-3000
Web: astrazeneca.com

Highlights

- U.S. President/CEO: David R. Brennan
- Annual Revenue: $17.8 billion
- R&D 2002: $2.6 billion
- Sales Force Size: 6000
- Number of employees: 50,000 worldwide
- Operating in countries worldwide: 100
- Corporate headquarters are in London and research headquarters are in Sweden.
- Opened a state-of-the-art research center in Waltham, MA
- Formed an alliance with Incyte Pharmaceuticals, Oct. 1999.

- Manufactures products in 20 countries and has 5 major research centers.
- They produce Losec/Prilosec which is the top selling pharmaceutical product of all time.
- Novadex is the most prescribed breast cancer therapy and their Seloken is the world's leading cardioselective beta-blocker.
- Over 10,000 people work in the R&D department.
- Over 150 ongoing projects and 59 new chemical products in the pipeline.

Major Products & Therapeutic Areas

Oncology	Cardiovascular	Cardiovascular Combination	Central Nervous System
Nolvadex: breast cancer	Seloken: leading cardioselective beta-blocker	Lexxel, Logimax, Nif-Ten, Tenorectic, Unimax, and Zestoretic: + diuretic for hypertension	Seroque: schizophrenia
Arimidex: breast cancer			Zomig/rapimelt: acute treatment of migraine
Casodex: prostate cancer	Sular, Atacand, Canef, Imdur, Inderal, Plendil, Ramace, Tenormin and Zestril: hypertension	Crestor: cholesterol	Mysoline
Tomudex			Vivalan
Zoladex; Iressa			
Faslodex: breast cancer	Torpol-XL: hypertension/CHF		Inderal: migraine

Gastrointestinal	Anti-Infective	Pain and Anesthesia	Respiratory
Prilosec: acid-reducer	Apatef/Cefotan: bacterial infections	Duranest: long-acting anesthetic for surgery	Symbicort; Pulmicort: asthma/COPD
Nexium: acid-reducer		Carbocaine; Citanest	Rhinocort: rhinitis
Entocort: Chrohn's Disease	Merrem/Meronem	Diprivan; EMLA	Bambec/Bricanyl
		Marcaine, Xylocaine	Oxis
		Naropin	Accolate: asthma

Pipeline Products

Cardio-vascular	Gastro-intestinal	Oncology/Metabolic	Respiratory	Pain Control	Central Nervous Sys.	Anti-Infective
Exanta: clotting Cerovive: stroke	Rofleponide AZD3355	Iressa: cancer Galida: diabetes	Symbicort Turbuhaler	Diprivan AZD4282	Seroquel AZD0947	AZD2563

Aventis Pharma

300 Somerset
Corporate Blvd.
Bridgewater, NJ
08807-2854
Phone: 908-231-4000
Phone: 800-981-2491
Web: aventis.com

Highlights

- Chief Executive Officer: Richard J. Markham
- Annual Revenue: $16.6 billion
- R&D 2002: $2.97 billion
- Sales Force Size: 5,200 (20,000 global)
- Number of employees: 71,000 worldwide
- Operating in countries worldwide: 100
- Company was formed by the merger of Hoechst Marion Roussel and Rhone-Poulenc Rorer in 1999.
- Aventis and Pfizer have confirmed co-effort on long-term Exubera studies, October 14, 2002.
- Ranks #1 in global vaccine market.
- Collaboration agreement with ImmunoGen in July 2003.
- Signed Licensing deal with Dainippon for new cognitive enhancer in August 2003.
- Aventis ranks second in the global biologicals market, third in the cardiovascular diseases and diabetes and diabetes and fourth in anti-infectives and allergy/asthma.
- Aventis Behring is based in the United States and is currently known as Centeon, a manufacturer of therapeutic proteins.
- Have 5,600 scientist and support personnel in R&D departments.
- Over 60 promising projects in the pipeline.

Major Products & Therapeutic Areas

Anti-Inflammatory	Anti-Infectives	Metabolic	Gastrointestinal	Neuroscience
Arava: "disease modifying" for rheumatoid arthritis	Synercid: life threatening infections	Amaryl: Type II diabetes	Carafate: duodenal ulcers	Anzemet: post-operative nausea and vomiting
	Ketek			
	Claforan: broad spectrum antibiotic	DiaBeta and Lantus: Type I & II diabetes		Rilutek: ALS
				Copaxone: MS
	Tavanic: antibiotic	Lasix: edema		

Cardiovascular	Respiratory	Oncology	Women's Health	Specialty
Lovenox: deep vein thrombosis	Allegra/Allegra D: allergy symtoms	Taxotere: breast and lung cancer	Actonel: post-menopausal osteoporosis	DDAVP: bed wetting
Trenatal: increased blood flow	Azmacort Inhaler: asthma	Nilandron: prostate cancer		
Refluden: anti-coagulant	Nasacort AQ/Nasocort Nasal Inhaler: allergy symptoms	Campto: colorectal cancer		
Delix: hypertension				

Pipeline Products

Metabolic	Metabolic	Respiratory	Specialty	Specialty
Acton-Euro	Exubera: inhalable insulin	Ketolid	Gene-activated erythropoetin (GA-EPO)	Genasense: cancer
Insulin glargine		Cidesonide: asthma		

Bausch & Lomb

1400 N. Goodman Street
P.O. Box 30450
Rochester, NY 14603–0450
Phone: 716-338-6000
Web: bausch.com

Highlights

- Chairman/CEO: Ronald L. Zarrella
- Annual Revenue: $1.8 billion
- R&D 2002: $128.4 million
- Sales Force Size: 200
- Number of employees: 11,500 worldwide
- Operating in countries worldwide: 35
- Founded in 1853 by John Jacob Bausch, a German immigrant and Henry Lomb.
- Headquartered in Rochester, New York.
- Products are available in 100 countries around the globe.

- Company has three product lines: Vision Care, Surgical and Pharmaceuticals.
- Bausch & Lomb offs the most comprehensive line of eye care products.
- Market drugs for the following conditions: Glaucoma, Eye Allergies, Conjunctivitis and Dry Eye.
- Celebrated 150th anniversary in 2003.

Major Products & Therapeutic Areas

Anti-Inflammatory	Allergy	Vitamins	Glaucoma
Lotemax: steroid suspension for post-op use and conjunctivitis	Alrez: first corticosteroid specifically for seasonal allergic conjunctivitis	Ocuvite/Ocuvite Extra: for healthy eyes	OptiPranolol: topical blocker for open-angle glaucoma or ocular hypertension
Indocollyre: non-steroid		Ocuvite Lutein: nutritional support of the eyes.	

Specialty	Equipment	Specialty	Specialty
Muro 128: corneal edema	Technolas 217z Zyoptix: vision correction	Technolas 217A Excimer Laser Systems: Hyperopias Astigmatism	Vitrasert: drug delivery implant
		Carteol: non-selective beta blocker	

Pipeline Products

Surgery	Specialty	Specialty	Specialty
Zyoptix system: personalized laser vision correction	Envision TD: age-related macular dengeration	Fluocinolone Acetonide Implant: diabetic macular edema	

Bayer Corporation

Pharmaceutical Division
400 Morgan Lane
West Haven, CT 06516
Phone: 203-812-2000
Web: bayer.com

Highlights

- Chairman/CEO: Global Board of Management
- Annual Revenue: $28 billion
- R&D 2002: $2.4 billion
- Sales Force Size: 2500
- Number of employees: 122,600 worldwide
- Operating in countries worldwide: 150
- Owned by Bayer AG, a $30.6 billion dollar company based in Leverkusen, Germany consisting of 350 companies.
- Acquired Visible Genetics, October 14 2002.
- Portfolio consists of approximately 10,000 products.
- Business relationships with Milennium Pharmaceuticals, LION BioScience and CuraGen.
- Spent $80 million on research facility expansion in 1999.

- Fourteen substances in phase I or II clinical trials and twenty-four in preclinical development.
- Health group accounts for 1/4 of total sales.
- Signed an agreement with Avigen, Inc. in Nov. 2000 granting Bayer worldwide marketing and distribution rights for Coagulin-B, a gene therapy treatment for Hemophilia B.
- One of four companies with plasma fractionation technology.
- Pharmaceutical focus on: antibiotics, metabolic, cardiovasular and hemophilia.
- Cipro, #1 quinolone. Named "Drug of the Century" by *Med Ad News*.
- Spends 100 million/year on employee education.

Major Products & Therapeutic Areas

Anti-Infectives	Metabolic	Cardiovascular	Specialty
Avelox: respiratory	Precose: Type I and II diabetes	Adalat C: hypertension	Trasylol: reduces blood loss during coronary bypass surgery
Cipro: quinolone		Baycol: lipid lowering	
Biltricide: schistosoma species			Levitra: erectile dysfunction

Anti-Viral/Immune	Hematology	Respiratory	Oncology
Gamimune N.	Kogenate: blood clotting	Prolastin: genetic emphysema	Viadur: once yearly treatment for prostate cancer
Thrombate III			

Pipeline Products

Anti-Viral/Immune	Hematology	Urology	Specialty
ICAM: common cold	Kogenate 3: hemophilia	Levitra:erectile dysfunction	
	Gene therapy: Factor III		

Berlex Laboratories, Inc.

340 Changebridge Road
P.O. Box 1000
Montville, NJ 07045-1000
Phone: 973-487-2000
Web: berlex.com

Highlights

- Chairman/CEO: Reinhard Franzen
- Annual Revenue: $1.5 billion
- R&D 2002: $255 million (approx.)
- Sales Force Size: 900
- Number of employees: 2000 worldwide
- Operating in countries worldwide: 100
- Schering AG, Germany, is the parent company.
- Entered U.S. market in 1979 when Berlex acquired part of the Internal Medicine division of Cooper Laboratories.
- 21 marketed products.
- Reserach facilities were consolidated in Rich mond, CA by 1993. Pipeline projects: 100.
- Berlex introduced all of the following products first:
  1. Magnetic Resonance Imaging Agent
  2. Therapy for Chronic Lymphocytic Leukemia
  3. Seven-day estrogen replacement therapy
  4. Multiple Sclerosis therapy
  5. Organ-specific imaging agent.
- Berlex has three operating divisions:
  1. Berlex Biosciences
  2. Berlex Drug Development & Technology
  3. Berlex Laboratories
- National Healthcare Alliances Group focuses on the needs of institutional customers.

Major Products & Therapeutic Areas

Women's Health	Women's Health	Diagnostic Imaging	Diagnostic Imaging
Mirena: intrauterine device	Levlen 21/Levlin 28; TriLevlen 21/TriLevlen 28; Yasmin: oral contraceptives	Feridex I.V.: first organ specific imaging agent in the U.S.	Neotect; Magnevist; Acutect; Ultravist: radiodiagnostic product
Climara: 7 day transdermal estrogen replacement therapy and osteoporosis treatment.	Levlite: low-dose estrogen		Feridex

Dermatology/Other	Oncology	Neurology	Cardiovascular
Leverlan/Kerastick: first PDT for treatment of actinic keratosis	Campath: B-cell chronic lymphocytic leukemia	Betaseron: SC injectable for multiple sclerosis	Betapace/Betapace AF: atrial fibrillation & atrial flutter
Finacea Gel: rosacea	Fludara: leukemia		Refludan: HIT- heparin-induced thrombocytopenia
Maxair Inhaler: asthma	Quadramet: bone cancer		
	Leukine: AML		Quinaglute: antiarrhyth

Pipeline Products

Women's Health	Diagnostic Imaging	Therapeutics	Dermatology/Oncology
Climara Pro: menopausal	Resovist: magnetic imaging	HPV Vaccine	
Climarelle/Yasmin 20			

Boehringer Ingelheim

900 Ridgebury Road
Ridgefield, CT 06877
Phone: 203-798-9988
Web: Boehringer-Ingelheim.com

Highlights

- Chairman/CEO: J. Martin Carroll-Jan. 2003
- Annual Revenue: $7.2 billion
- R&D 2002: $1.23 billion
- Sales Force Size: 1200
- Number of employees: 33,000 worldwide
- Operating in countries worldwide: 60
- Privately owned company founded in Ingelheim, Germany 115 years ago and the world base of operations is still located there. They have 143 affiliated companies.
- CQIA Innovation Prize-Viramune, July 2002.
- Have more than 42 research and development sites and employs 3,000 scientists.

- Sales of human pharmaceuticals represents 96% of their total sales.
- Acquired Pharmaton, a phytomedicines specialist company in 1991.
- Acquired BenVenue, an injectable and hospital product manufacturer in 1997.
- Launched Combivent in 1996, Flomax in 1997, and Mobic in 1999 followed by Viramune.
- Co-markets Miracles with GlaxoSmithKline.
- Received FDA approval for Cafcit in 2000.
- Will co-promote Spiriva with Pfizer.
- One of the top 20 pharmaceutical companies.

Major Products & Therapeutic Areas

Respiratory	Respiratory	Cardiovascular	Cardiovascular
Combivent: COPD	Berodual/Duovent: COPD, Asthma, & Emphysema	Micardis/Plus: hypertension Aggrenox: stroke	Actilyse: MI/stroke
Atrovent: COPD			Mexitil: antiarrhythmia
Alupent: asthma	Berotec: CFC-Free Inhaler	Catapres/Catapres TTS: hypertension	Persantine: platelet inhibitor
Spiriva: COPD			Metalyse: acute MI

Anti-Viral/ Immune System	Musculoskeletal	Neuroscience	Urology/ Specialty
Viramune: HIV-1	Mobic: non-steroidal anti-infammatory for osteo-arthritis, rheumatoid arthritis, and ankylosing spondylitis.	Mirapex: Parkinson's	Flomax: BPH
		Serentil	Caficit

Pipeline Products

Respiratory	Neuroscience	Oncology	Anti-Viral/Immune	Specialty
	Domin, Fibanserin and Talsaclidine	Promycin	Tipranavir	Marinol
	NS 2330: Alzheimer's/ Parkinson's			KUC 7483: urge urinary incontinence

Bristol-Myers Squibb CO

345 Park Avenue
New York, NY 10154-0037
Phone: 212-546-4000
Web: bms.com

Highlights

- Chairman/CEO: Peter R. Dolan
- Annual Revenue: $18.1 billion
- R&D 2002: $2.1 billion
- Sales Force Size: 5,200
- Number of employees: 44,000 worldwide
- Operating in countries worldwide: 60
- Sold Clairol Hair Products division to Proctor and Gamble in 2001.
- Peter S. Ringrose, PhD is CSO and President of Bristol-Myers Squibb Pharmaceutical Research Institute.

- BMS has 64 product lines.
- Partner with Imclone for Erbitux, Aug. 2003.
- **Acquired DuPont in October 2001.**
- Received the National Medal of Technology in 1999.
- More than 50 compounds in the pipeline.
- Top 10 Companies for Working Mothers 2002.
- BMS has 29 products with global sales over $100 million each.
- BMS created a new orthopedic division in 2001. This division is the Zimmer division.
- Other divisions: ConvaTec, Mead Johnson, Oncology Therapeutics Network.

Major Products & Therapeutic Areas

Oncology	Cardiovascular	Metabolic	Neuroscience
Taxol: testicular, ovarian and colorectal cancer	Pravachol: cholesterol	Glucovance/ Glucophage XR + HTZD: Type II diabetes	Buspar: anti-anxiety
	Avalide		Serzone: anti-depressant
Ifex	Avapro: hypertension	Metaglip: Type II diabetes	Lodosyn
Paraplatin	Monopril/Monpril- HCT: hypertension		Sinemet CR
			Abilify: schizophrenia

Infectious Disease	Women's Health	Medical Imaging	Specialty
Duricef; Sustiva	Estrace: HRT	Cardiolite	Plavix/Plavix + aspirin: platelet aggregation inhibitor
Azactam: Videx EC	FemTone	Miraluma	
Cefzil; Zerit	Vaniqa	Definity	Avapro: diabetic neuropathy
Fungizone/ Reyataz			Coumadin: platelet inhibitor
Tequin/Trimox			

Pipeline Products

Cardiovascular/Infectious	Neuroscience	Anti-Viral/Anti-AIDS	Oncology
Vanlev: hypertension/ CHF	CTRLA4-Ig (RA & MS)	Entecavir: Hepatitis B	Erbitux: cancer
CRF1 antagonist: depression	Factor Xa Inhibitor: deep vein thrombosis anticoagulant	Atazanavir: HIV	Taxane: tumors
Garenoxacin: antibiotic		Ravuconazole: fungal infection	Epothilone: multiple tumors

Elan Pharmaceuticals

300 Gateway Blvd.
S. San Francisco, CA 94080
Phone: 650-877-0900
Web: elan.com

Highlights

- President/CEO: Kelly Martin
- Annual Revenue: $1.4 billion ($2.4 bil. loss)
- R&D 2003: $114 million
- Sales Force Size: 1000
- Number of employees: 2,900 worldwide
- Operating in countries worldwide: 35
- Founded in 1969.
- Headquartered in Dublin, Ireland.
- Acquired the Liposome Company, May 2000.
- Sold Actiq rights to Cephalon for $50 million.
- Collaborates with Biogen, Inc.
- Recovery Plan: Primary Care Franchise Sale
- Acquired Quadrant Heathcare, a company specializing in protein and peptide delivery research in December 2000.
- Merged with Dura Pharmaceuticals, Inc. in November 2000.
- Acquired Carnrick Laboratories and Neurex Corporation in 1998.
- Acquired Athena Neurosciences, Inc. in 1996.
- Has 27 pipeline drugs currently in different phases of clinical trials.
- 1000 employees work in research and development.
- Sold franchise rights to Sonata and Skelaxin in January 2003. Reached settlement agreement with King for these products in May 2003.

Major Products & Therapeutic Areas

Pain Management	Anti-Inflammatory	Anti-Infective	Cardiovascular
Skelaxin: musculoskeletal pain	Naprelan: osteoarthritis and rheumatoid arthritis	Abelcet: fungal infections	Corlopam
Myobloc		Azactam: bacterial	
Zanaflex	Zanaflex: spastic muscle	Maxipime: bacterial	
Roxicodone (oxycodone)			

Neuroscience	Neuroscience	Dermatology	Diagnostic
Zonegran: epileptic seizures	Mysoline: epilepsy and seizure disorders	Aclovate	Elan offers over 50 diagnostic neurological testing services.
		Cutivate	
Permax: Parkinson's	Myobloc: cervical dystonia	Emgel	
Diastat: epileptic cluster seizures		Oxistat	
		Temovate	

Pipeline Products

Neuroscience	Neuroscience	Neuroscience	Other
Zonegran: migraine & mania	Zelapar: Parkinson's	Prialt: chronic severe pain	
	Antegren: MS & Crohn's	ELU-154088: pain	

159

Eli Lilly and Company

Lilly Corporate Center
Indianapolis, IN 46285
Phone: 317-276-2000
Web: lilly.com

Highlights

- Chairman/CEO: Sidney Taurel
- Annual Revenue: $11 billion
- R&D 2003: $2.15 billion
- Sales Force Size: 13,500 (5,200 in U.S.)
- Number of employees: 43,000 worldwide
- Operating in countries worldwide: 146
- Founded by Colonel Eli Lilly in 1876 in Indianapolis, Indiana
- *Industry Week Magazine* recognized Lilly as "One of the World's Best-Managed Companies" in August 2000.
- *Fortune Magazine* ranks Lilly among the top "Companies for Working Mothers" and among "100 Best Companies to Work For."
- Formed alliances with Takeda Pharmaceuticals and Ribozyme Pharmaceuticals, Inc.
- Has approximately 60 products in the pipeline.
- **Expects to launch 9 blockbuster drugs by the end of 2004.** Have 8,300 R&D employees.
- Plan to increase their sales force by 5000 over the next three years.
- Lilly is offering a $12 flat fee per prescription for senior citizens in need of assistance.

Major Products & Therapeutic Areas

Metabolic	Women's Health	Specialty	Cardiovascular
Actos: Type II diabetes	Evista: osteoporosis	Humatrope: growth hormone deficiency	ReoPro: cardiac ischemic complications
Humulin & Humalog Pen		Xigris: adult severe sepsis	
Humalog rapid acting			

Oncology	Gastrointestinal	Neuroscience	Neuroscience
Gemzar: pancreatic, non-small-cell lung cancer and breast cancer	Axid: ulcers & heartburn	Prozac: depression, OC disorder and bulimia	Sarafem: PMDD
			Strattera: ADHD
		Zyprexa: schizophrenia	

Pipeline Products

Other	Neuroscience	Neuroscience	Urology/Other
Xigris: severe sepsis	Prozac: weekly dose	Duloxetine: antidepressant	Cialis: erectile dysfunction
Alimta: cancer	Zyprexa: IM: schizophrenia		Exenatide: diabetes
PKC beta inhibitor: eyes			

Forest Laboratories, Inc.

900 Third Avenue
New York, NY 10022
Phone: 212-421-7850
Web: frx.com

Highlights

- Chairman/CEO: Howard Solomon
- Annual Revenue: $2.2 billion
- R&D 2002: $2 million
- Sales Force Size: 2300
- Number of employees: 4,600 worldwide
- Operating in countries worldwide: 35
- Markets products in the United States and Europe.
- Founded in 1956.
- Plans to increase sales force size in 2004.
- Forest has three sales divisions in the U.S. with a total of 2,300 sales force personnel.
  1. Forest Pharmaceuticals
  2. Forest Therapeutics
  3. Forest Specialty Sales
- Ranks 23rd on *Fortune Magazines* list of "100 Fastest Growing Companies."
- Forest promoted 25% of their sales force in the year 2000. They increased their total sales force by 70%.
- On **Selling Powers** "50 Best Companies to Sell For" for the years 2000-2002.
- In Top 100 "Hot Growth" Companies in U.S., 2001.
- Co-promotes Benicar with Sankyo Pharmaceuticals.
- Has 600 employees on scientific staff.

Major Products & Therapeutic Areas

Respiratory	Neuroscience	Anti-Infectives	Women's Health
Aeobid: asthma	Celexa: depression	Monurol: urinary tract infections	Cervidil: obstetrical
Infasurf: for infants	Lexapro: depression-launch September, 2002.		

Cardiovascular	Specialty	Other	Other
Tiazac: hypertension	Thyrolar:Thyroid abd.		
Benicar: hypertension	Armous: Thyroid/ Levothyroid		

Pipeline Products

Respiratory/ Gastrointestinal	Neuroscience	Women's Health	Pain/Cardiovascular
Aerobid HFA & Aerospan non-CFC: asthma	Escitalopram: depression	Climara Pro: hormone replacement therapy	Oxycodone/ibuprofen: add indications
Dexloxiglumide: IBS/ Constipation	Memantine: Alzheimer's		Tiazac/Lexcanidipine: hypertension
	Neramexare		

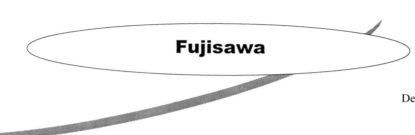

Fujisawa

Parkway North Center
3 Parkway N.
Deerfield, IL 60015-2548
Phone: 847-317-8800
Web: fujisawa.com

Highlights

- Chairman/CEO: Global Board of Management
- Annual Revenue: $2.5 billion
- R&D 2003: 15% of total sales
- Sales Force Size: 200
- Number of employees: 8,000 worldwide
- Operating in countries worldwide: 30
- Subsidiary of Fujisawa Pharmaceutical Company, Ltd. based in Osaka, Japan.
- Parent company was founded in 1894.

- Research facilities located in Japan, North America, Europe and Asia.
- Atrix acquires marketing rights for Atrisone.
- Ethical pharmaceuticals are 90% of Fujisawa's business.
- June 2003, will co-promote Protopic with GSK.
- Signed license agreement with Daiichi Santory Pharma to develop and market carperitide for treatment of acute heart failure in June 2003.

Major Products & Therapeutic Areas

Anti-Infectives	Cardiovascular	Dermatology	Transplantation
AmBisome: fungal infections	Adenocard: antiarrhythmic agent	Protopic: eczema; atopic dermatitis in children	Prograf: organ rejection
Cefizox	Adenoscan: diagnostic	Cyclocort	
Aristocort		Atrisone	

Specialty	Other	Other	Other
Ansyr Syringe: needleless			

Pipeline Products

Anti-Infectives	Cardiovascular	Dermatology	Specialty
AmBisome: add ind.		Protopic: add. indications	Prograf: add. ind

Genentech, Inc.

1 DNA Way
S. San Francisco, CA
Phone: 650-225-1000
Web: genentech.com

Highlights

- Chairman/CEO: Arthur D. Levinson, PhD.
- Annual Revenue: $3 billion (approx.)
- R&D 2003: 23% of revenues
- Sales Force Size: 1100
- Number of employees: 4,500 worldwide
- Operating in countries worldwide: 100
- Founded April 7, 1976 by Herb Boyer and Bob Swanson.
- A top biotechnology company that has produced twelve of their approved biotechnology products; has 20 projects in pipeline as of August 2003.
- Genentech receives royalties from Roche for sale of their products in Canada/Europe.

- Genentech holds more than 4300 patents worldwide and has over 5000 others pending.
- Has more than 700 scientists. These scientists publish at a rate of approximately 275 scientific papers per year.
- Plans to launch six new products in 2003.
- Made *Working Mother Magazine's* "100 Best Companies" for the 10th time and *Fortune's* "100 Best..." List again in January 2003.
- August 2003, settled patent dispute with Amgen.
- Rituxan: #1 selling anti-tumor drug in U.S., 2003.
- Partners with Novartis and Tanox.

Major Products & Therapeutic Areas

Metabolic/Hormone	Plasma/Antibody	Cardiovascular	Oncology
Nutropin & Nutropin AQ: growth hormone treatment for GHD and Turner syndrome	Protropin: growth hormone for children	Activase: acute MI, pulmonary embolism, and ischemic stroke	Herceptin: metastic breast cancer
	Pulmozyme: cystic fibrosis	TNKase: acute MI	Rituxan: non-Hodgkin's lymphoma
Nutropin Depot: growth hormone		Tracleer: arterial hypertension	Avastin: renal cell carcinoma

Respiratory	Immune Systems	Gastrointestinal	Specialty
Xolair: allergic asthma and allergic rhinitis	Xanelim: psoriasis and kidney transplant rejection	LDP-02: IBS	AMD Fab: age-related macular degeneration
INS365 Respiratory: chronic bronchitis			Neutropin Depot: add. Indications

Pipeline Products

Cardiovascular	BioOncology	BioOncology	Immunological
Lucentis	Tarceva: non-small cell lung cancer Avastin	Omnitary	Rituxan Ab/MLN-02 Ab
Veletri		Herceptin Antibody	Xolair
	Rituxan: non-Hodgkin's		Raptiva

GlaxoSmithKline

Five Moore Drive
P.O. Box 13398
Research Triangle Park, NC
27709
Phone: 888-825-5249
Web: gsk.com

Highlights

- Chairman/CEO: Jean-Pierre Garnier
- Annual Revenue: $31.8 billion
- R&D 2002: $4 billion
- Sales Force Size: 40,000
- Number of employees: 100,000 worldwide
- Operating in countries worldwide: 150
- Have more than 60 products and 99 manufacturing sites in 39 countries.
- **Largest research-based** pharmaceutical company in the world. R & D Employees: 16,000
- August 2003- copromote Vesicare with Yamanouchi.

- GSK formed December 27, 2000 by merger of Glaxo Wellcome and SmithKlineBeecham.
- GSK had four products with sales over $1 billion each and 16 products with sales in excess of $500 million each .
- GSK donates more than $90 million in cash to needy communities around the world.
- First human trails with recombinant, adjuvanted candidate HIV vaccine started January 31, 2002.
- Sales force ranked #1 by these physician groups according to Scott-Levin, 2001: GP, FP, Pediatricians and Pulmonologists.
- July 2003, CorixaCorp and GSK will copromote Bexxar.

Major Products & Therapeutic Areas

Anti-Virals	Cardiovascular/ Gastrointestinal	Neuroscience	Neuroscience
Relenza: influenza	Lanoxin	Zyban, Seroxat/Paxil: anxiety and post-traumatic stress syndrome	Amerge: migraine
Zovirax: malaria	Trandate		Imitrex: migraine
Malarone: malaria	Zantac: ulcers	Paxil CR: depression/ anxiety	Lamictal: epilepsy
Trizivir: HIV	Lotronex: IBS		WellbutrinSR: depression
Valtrex: HSV			

Metabolic/Oncology	Vaccines	Respiratory	Anti-Infectives/ Urology
Avandia/Avandamet: Diabetes	Twinrix: hepatitis A&B	Beclovent, Beconase, Exosurf Neonatal, Flonase, Flovent and Flovent ROTADISK: asthma & COPD; Serevent DISKUS and Serevent: asthma; Advair: asthma/ped., Ventolin: asthma & COPD	Ceftin
	Engerrix-B: hepatitis B		Fortax
Navelbine	Havrix: hepatitis A		Zinacef
Zofran	Infanrix DTP: absorbed		Levitra: erectile dys.
Bexxar: cancer	LYMErix: lyme disease		Vesicare: OAB: urinary frequency

Pipeline Products

Anti-Infectives	Oncology/Neuroscience	Oncology/Neuroscience	Respiratory
Ziagen/Epivil: HIV Relenza: flu; Zefflix: Hep. B	Eniluracil/Panorex/Hycamtin: cancer	Avodart: prostate cancer ReQuip: Parkinson's Lamictal: pain/bipolar	Flovent/Ariflo: COPD; Flixonase: sinusitis

Johnson & Johnson

One Johnson and Johnson Plaza
New Brunswick, NJ 08993
Phone: 732-524-0400
Web: jnj.com

Highlights

- Chairman/CEO: William C. Weldon
- Annual Revenue: $36.3 billion
- R&D 2002: $3 billion
- Sales Force Size: 5000
- Number of employees: 110,900 worldwide
- Operating in countries worldwide: 175
- Founded by Robert Wood Johnson and his brothers in 1886.
- Headquartered in New Brunswick.
- Johnson & Johnson employs more than 40,000 people in the United States.
- Johnson & Johnson products are too numerous to list. They must be researched under the different divisions. This is true for the pipeline products as well.
- Contributes more than $215 million annually to social and environmental products.
- Acquired ALZA Corporation in 2001.
- Ranked 4th in *Business Week*'s top "50 Best-Performing Companies."
- Johnson & Johnson consists of 190 operating companies.
- Acquired Tibotec-Virco, a Biopharmaceutical Company in 2002.

Johnson & Johnson Company Divisions

Centocor, Inc.
Johnson & Johnson Clinical Diagnostics, Inc.
Cordis Corporation
Johnson & Johnson Health Care Systems, Inc.
DePuy, Inc.
R. W. Johnson Pharmaceutical Research Institute
Ethicon Endo-Surgery, Inc.
Ortho Biotec, Inc.
Indigo Medical, Inc.
Ortho-Clinical Diagnostics
Ethicon, Inc.
Ortho-Dermatological
Advanced Sterilization Products
Ortho-McNeil Pharmaceuticals, Inc.
Johnson & Johnson Medical, Inc.
Therakos
Janssen Pharmaceutica, Inc.
Vistakon

To see a complete list of Johnson & Johnson Company websites:
jnj.com/who_is_jnj/opsites_index.html

Merck & Co., Inc.

One Merck Drive
P.O. Box 100
Whitehouse Station, NJ 08889
Phone: 908-423-1000
Web: merck.com

Highlights

- Chairman/CEO: Raymond V. Gilmartin
- Annual Revenue: $33 billion
- R&D 2002: $2.9 billion
- Sales Force Size: 5000
- Number of employees: >77,000 worldwide
- Operating in countries worldwide: 150
- Merck is a New Jersey based pharmaceutical company.
- It's ranked the second largest pharmaceutical company in the United States.
- *The Merck Manual* is produced by Merck and it is the most widely used medical text in the world. Over 300 experts contribute infor mation to *The Merck Manual.*
- Merck acquired Rosetta Inpharmatics, Inc. a leading informational genomics company on May 11, 2001.
- Merck expects to add 1,500 new sales representatives to their sales force in the United States within the year.
- Merck has 11 major research centers.
- Expected to launch 11 new medicines and vaccines between 2002 and 2006.

Major Products & Therapeutic Areas

Anti-Inflammatory	Anti-Infectives	Cardiovascular	Immune Response	Respiratory
Vioxx: arthritis	Cancidas: fungal	Aggrastat: angina	Propecia: male pattern baldness	Singulair: maintenance therapy for asthma/ allergic rhinitis
Arcoxia: OS/RA/ gout	Crixivan: HIV	Cozaar & Hyzaar: hypertension		
	Mefoxin			
	Noroxin	Zocor: cholesterol		
	Primaxin	Zetia: cholesterol		
	Invanz: bacterial			

Endocrinology	Gastroenterology	Neurological	Ophthalmic	Vaccines
Fosamax: osteoporosis	Prilosec & Nexium: acid reducer; ulcers	Maxalt: migraine	Cosopt	Comvax: Hep. B
		Sinemet	Trusopt	M-M-R II
Proscar: enlarged prostate		Sinemet CR	Timoptic	B PNEUMOVAX 23
			Timoptic-XE	RECOMBIVAX HB
				VAQTA: hepatitis A
				VARIVAX: varicella

Pipeline Products

Neurological/Other	Anti-Infectives/Other	Vaccines	Metabolic/ Anti-Inflammatory
Aprepitant: depression	Invanz: resistant infections	Rotavirus Vaccine	MK-767: diabetes
Emend: chemo-induced nausea/vomiting	RotaTeq: infant diarrhea	HPV: genital warts	KRP-297: Type II diabetes
	Herpes Zoster Vaccine	HIV: HIV/AIDS	Zocor/ Zetia: cholesterol

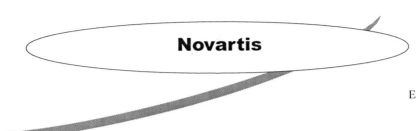

Novartis

59 Route 10
P.O. Box 11
East Hanover, NJ 07936
Phone: 973-781-8300
Web: novartis.com

Highlights

- Chairman/CEO: Daniel Vasella
- Annual Revenue: $20.9 billion
- R&D 2002: $2.8 billion
- Sales Force Size: 13,000
- Number of employees: 72,900 worldwide
- Operating in countries worldwide: 140
- Novartis represents the $27 billion merger of Ciba-Geigy and Sandox Pharmaceuticals.
- Geneva Pharmaceuticals, CIBA Vision, SyStemix, Inc. and GTI, Inc. are all part of Novartis.

- Novartis employs 7,000 people in the United States and 3,000 of those people are in the United States sales force.
- Obtained 15 FDA product approvals in 2001.
- Submitted 18 new drug applications.
- Added more than 1,000 new R&D employees.
- U.S. market represents 43% of pharmaceutical sales.
- As of October 2002, Novartis had 67 projects in clinical development with 30 of those projects in late stage development.

Major Products & Therapeutic Areas

Bone/ Inflammation/Other	Cardiovascular/ Metabolic	Dermatology/ Hematology	Neuroscience
Miacalcin: mineral homeostasis and skeletal metabolism	Diovan/Diovan HCT, Lotrel, Lotensin/Lotensin HCT: hypertension	Lamisil: fungal infections of the skin and nails	Stalevoil: Parkinson's
Famvir: herpes	Lescol: cholesterol	Elidel: eczema	Trileptal: anti-convulsant
Voltaren: arthritis	Starlix: Type II diabetes	Neoral	
Visudyne: (AMD)		Sandoglobulin: immuno-defiency	
Xolair: allergic asthma			

Neuroscience	Oncology/Respiratory	Transplantation	Women's Health/Other
Exelon: Alzheimer's	Zometa, Aredia: cancer	Neoral/Sandimmune: prevent graft rejection	Estraderm: post-menopausal estrogen deficiency
Comtan: Parkinson's	Femara: breast cancer		
Clozaril: schizophrenia	Sandostatin/Sandostatin LAR: acromegaly/cancer	Simulet: acute organ rejection in kidney transplants	HRT Range: osteoporosis
Tegretol: epilepsy			Zelmac/Zelnormin: IBS
Mellaril, Ritalin/Ritalin SR: ADHD & Narcolepsy	Glivec/Gleevec: GI tumors/ CML		Foradil: asthma (LA)

Pipeline Products

Neuroscience	Oncology/ Neuroscience	Bone/Inflammation	Cardiovascular/ Gastrointestinal
Trileptal: epilepsy	Letrozole: breast cancer	Zoledronate: osteoporosis	Revasc: acute coronary syndrome
Exelon: Alzheimer's	Migranal: migraines	Zometa: bone testing	Zelmec: IBS/reflux

Novo Nordisk

405 Lexington Avenue
Suite 6400
New York, NY 10017
Phone: 212-867-0123
Web: novonordisk.com

Highlights

- Chairman/CEO: Lars Rebien Sorensen
- Annual Revenue: $2.6 billion
- R&D 2002: $410 million
- Sales Force Size: 3,700 (700 U.S.)
- Number of employees: 18,221 worldwide
- Operating in countries worldwide: 68
- Novo was founded in the early 1920s.
- Novo Nordisk was formed by the merger of Novo and Nordisk in 1989.
- Healthcare products produce 75% of revenues.

- Novo Nordisk has one of the largest diabetes product portfolios in the healthcare industry.
- More than 70% of Novo Nordisk's sales are diabetic products.
- Novo Nordisk's Diabetic Research Division is named Protein Delivery.

Major Products & Therapeutic Areas

Metabolic	Metabolic	Metabolic	Immunology
Actrapid	Insulatard	All of the products listed under the Metabolic category are forms of insulin for the treatment of diabetes.	NovoSeven: Hemophilia A and B
Lente	Mixtard		
Monotard	Prandin		
Actraphane	Glucagen		
Protaphane	NovoNorm/GlucoNorm	NovoMix30: Flexpen-U.S.	
Velosulin/Novolin	NovoRapid/NovoLog		

Growth Hormone	Hormone Replacement	Hormone Replacement	Delivery Systems
Norditropin/SimpleXx: hormone growth deficiency in children and adults	Activelle, Kliogest and Trisequens: HRT in post-menopausal women	Vagifem: vaginal dryness	InDuo
			FlexPen
			Innovo/ InnoLet
NordipenXx/ Nordipenmate Xx: delivery systems	Estrofem: estrogen replacement for women who have had a hysterectomy		NovoPen Junior
			NovoPen/ NovoLet
			NovoFine Needles

Pipeline Products

Metabolic	Immunology	Gastroenterology	Other
NovoMix 50/70: insulin	NovoSeven: liver transplantation	NovoSeven: upper GI bleeds	Norditropin: new ind.
Insulin detemir (NN304)			

Organon, Inc.

375 Mt. Pleasant Avenue
West Oramge, NJ 07052
Phone: 973-325-4500
Web: organon.com

Highlights

- President (U.S.): Michael V. Novinski
- Annual Revenue: $2.45 billion
- R&D 2002: $465 million
- Sales Force Size: 4,000
- Number of employees: 13,000 worldwide
- Operating in countries worldwide: 50
- Organon started as a meat-processing firm based in the Netherlands in 1923.
- Today Organon is the largest Dutch research-based pharmaceutical company.
- Established new headquarters in U.S., 2002.

- Organon is the largest pharmaceutical business unit of Akzo Nobel.
- Organon is an expert in the field of hormone research and gynecology.
- **Organon regards its employees as its most valuable resource.**
- Organon produces *ORGYN*, a quarterly gynecological journal.
- Employees in Research & Development: 2,300
- Approximately, 120,000 gynecologists worldwide receive the *ORGYN* Journal.

Major Products & Therapeutic Areas

Cardiovascular	Contraception	Contraception	Neuroscience
Arixtra: thrombosis	Implanon: 3 yr implant	Marvelon/Desogen	Remeron: anti-depressant
	Laurina	Mercilon/Mircette	
	Nuva Ring: vaginal ring	Cerazette: estrogen-free	Remeron Sol. Tab- FD
		Gracial	

Anesthesia	Men's Health/ Women's Health	Fertility	HRT/Osteoporosis
Esmeron/Zemaron: anesthesia	Andriol: testosterone supplement	Orgalutran/Antagon	Livial
		Pregnyl	Ovestin
	Livial: menopausal symptoms	Purgeon/Follistim	Riselle
			Andriol

Pipeline Products

HRT/Osteoporosis	Fertility	Contraception/Other	Cardiovascular/ Immunology
(ERB) Second Estrogen Recptor	Orgalutran: GnRH for reproduction/infertility	Male Contraceptive	Orgaran: blood clot prevention
Livial: osteoporosis	Puregon: add. Indications	Contraceptive Vaginal Ring	HCgp-39: rheumatoid
		Xa inhibitors: thrombosis	

Ortho-McNeil

1000 Route # 202 South
Raritan, NJ 08869-0602
Phone: 908-218-6000
Web: ortho-mcneil.com

Highlights

- Chairman/CEO: see Johnson & Johnson
- Annual Revenue: see Johnson & Johnson
- R&D, year 2002: see Johnson & Johnson
- Sales Force Size: see Johnson & Johnson
- Number of employees: 3,500
- Operating in countries worldwide: 175
- McNeil was founded in 1878.
- Ortho was formed in the 1940s.
- Ortho marketed their first birth control pill in 1963.

- The Fund for Podiatric Medical Education (FPME) awarded Ortho-McNeil Pharmaceutical, Inc., marketer of **Regranex Gel** 0.01%, its ninth annual Corporate Citizen Award at the American Podiatric Medical Association's Annual Meeting in Philadelphia.
- Part of the 190 operating units of Johnson & Johnson.
- Ortho-McNeil Pharmaceutical, Inc. was formed by merger of Ortho and McNeil in 1993.

Major Products & Therapeutic Areas

Cardiovascular/ Anti-Infectives	Oral Contraceptives	Oral Contraceptives	Diaphragms/IUDs
Vascor: angina	Ortho Evra (TTS): first birth control patch	Ortho-Micronor	ALL-FLEX: diaphram
Floxin: anti-infective		Ortho-Novum	ORTHO: diaphram
Levaquin: anti-infective	Ortho Tri-Cyclen	Modicon	Paragard T 380A: IUD
	Ortho-Novumand	OrthoCept	
	OrthoCyclen		

Cystic Fibrosis/Wound	Neuroscience/ Urology	Women's Health	Pain Management
Pancrease Capsules	Topamax: epilepsy	Ortho: menopausal	Axert: migraine
Pancrease MT Capsules	Haldol: schizophrenia	Ortho Prefest: menopausal	Tolectin/Tylox
Regranex Gel: wound	Ditropan-XL/Elmiron: bladder spasm/pain		Tylenol, Tylenol with codeine
		ACI-JEL: vaginal jelly	
	Oitropan XL/ Elmieon: Urology	Sultrin: vaginal therapy	Ultracet/ Ultram
		Terazol: vaginal therapy	Parafon Forte

Pipeline Products

Reproductive Health	Anti-Infectives	Pain/Neuroscience	Pain/Neuroscience
Dapoxetine: premature or rapid ejaculation	Levaquin: chronic bacterial prostatitis	Topamax: migraine monotherapy	E Trans: acute post-operative pain

Pfizer Incorporated

235 East 42nd Street
New York, NY 10017-5755
Phone: 212-573-2323
Web: pfizer.com

Highlights

- Chairman/CEO: Henry A. McKinnell
- Annual Revenue: $32.4 billion
- R&D 2003: $7.1 billion
- Sales Force Size: 20,000
- Number of employees:120,000 worldwide
- Operating in countries worldwide: 150
- **Pfizer had the best sales force by physician audit six years in a row. Pfizer has eight of the top 30 selling medicines in the world.** Eight of these medicines are #1(*) in their therapeutic class and will earn more than $1 billion dollars each globally this year.
- Pfizer is a research-based, global pharmaceutical company that merged with Warner-Lambert.

- Health care market accounts for approximately 85% of its total sales. Pfizer co-promotes with Searle and Eisai Co.
- The U.S. pharmaceuticals group consists of: Alta, National Healthcare Operations, Pfizer Labs, Powers Rx, Pratt, Roerig, Specialty Division and Steere Pharmaceuticals.
- **Pfizer's Capsugel division is the world's largest producer of two-piece capsules for use with prescription and non-prescription medications. Pfizer has 200 potential new treatments and approximately 2 million compounds in their research library.**
- **Acquired Pharmacia** for $60 million in stock effective December, 2002.

Major Products & Therapeutic Areas

Cardiovascular	Infectious Diseases	Neuroscience	Anti-Inflammatory
*Lipitor: cholesterol	*Zithromax: antibiotic	*Zoloft: antidepressant	Celebrex: osteoarthritis and rheumatoid arthritis
*Norvasc: hypertension	Zyvox: hospital acq. infec.	*Neurontin: epilepsy	
Cardura: hypertension	Viracept/Rescriptor: HIV	Aricept: Alzheimer's	
Accupril: hypertension	*Diflucan: anti-fungal	Dilantin: seizures	Bextra: OA & RA
Tikosyn: atrial fibrillation	VFEND: anti-fungal	Ambien: insomnia	

Urology/Oncology	Metabolic/Allergies	Opthalmology/Other	Women's Health
*Viagra: erectile dys.	Zyrtec: indoor & outdoor allergies	*Xalatan: glaucoma	Loestrin/Estrostep: oral contraceptive
*Detrol/Detrol LA: overactive bladder	*Genotropin: growth disorders	Nicotrol: smoking cessation	Femhrt HRT: osteoporosis
Camptosar: metastatic colorectal cancer	Glucotrol XL: Type II diabetes	Relpax: migraine	

Pipeline Products

Cardiovascular	Neuroscience	Diabetes/Allergies	Infectious Disease/ Oncology
Atorvastatin: cholesterol	Donepezil: Alzheimer's	Inhaled Insulin: diabetes	Trovan: bacterial infec.
Candovatril: CHF	Varenicline: nicotine ad.	Reactine: antihistamine	Unasyn: anti-infective
Tikosyn: atrial fibrillation	Eletriptan: migraines	Alono: diabetic neuropathy	Drolovidene: advanced breast cancer
Xelide: cardiac arrhythmia	Zeldox: psychosis		

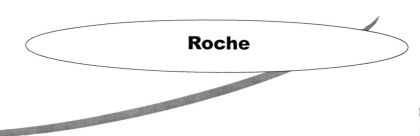

Roche

340 Kingsland St.
Nutley, NJ 07110
Phone: 973-235-5000
Web: roche.com

Highlights

- Chariman/CEO: Franz B. Humer
- Annual Revenue: $28 billion
- R&D 2002: $4 billion
- Sales Force Size: 5400
- Number of employees: 71,934 worldwide
- Operating in countries worldwide: 150
- Hoffman La Roche, Inc. was founded in 1896 in Basel, Switzerland.
- Pharmaceutical division accounts for over 60% of the Roche Group's sales.

- Ranked #1 company in the world in diagnostics.
- Acquired Boehringer Mannheim's Therapeutic Division and DePuy Orthopedics Company.
- Roche also has a majority holding in Genentech.
- Roche is an industry leader in hospital-based products.

Major Products & Therapeutic Areas

Cardiovascular	Neuroscience	Infectious Disease	Infectious Disease
Dilatrend: BD/CHF	Klonopin: sedative	Invirase: HIV	Bactrim; Cytovene; Gantrisin; Lariam; Rocephin and Trimpex: antibiotics
NeoRecormon: anemia	Romazicon	Tamiflu: Influenza	
Rapilysin: MI	Valium: sedative	Fortovase: HIV	
Activase: MI	Versed: nausea/anesthesia	Valcyte: HIV	Roferan-A: Hepatitis B and C
	Lexotan: anxiety	Pegasys: Hepatitis C	
		Viracept: HIV	

Inflammation/ Autoimmune	Metabolic/ Dermatology	Oncology	Organ Transplantation
Anaprox/ Naprosyn	Xenical: weight control	FUDR: colon cancer	CellCept: acute organ rejection
Toradol	Rocaltrol: Osteoporosis	Roferon-A	
Madopar: Parkinson's	Soriatane: dermatology	Xeloda: breast cancer	
Nutropin: Growth HD	Accutane: acne	Herceptin; Kytril; Rituxan	Zenapax: prevention of acute graft rejection
Pulmozyme: Cystic Fibrosis			

Pipeline Products

Oncology	Neuroscience	Metabolic/Oncology	Cardiovascular/ Infectious Disease
Rituxan: non-Hodgkin's lymphoma	Tasmar	Xenical: adolescent diabetes	Lamisiban: acute CS
Thymitaq: liver cancer	Tolcapone: Parkinson's	Mabthera: RA	Tenefuse: sepsis
Xeloda: colon cancer	Zalcose: diabetic neurophathy	Avastin: Chemo	

Sanofi-Synthelabo

90 Park Avenue
New York, NY 10016-1301
Phone: 212-551-4000
Web: sanofi-synthelabous.com

Highlights

- Chairman/CEO: Jean-Francois Dehecq
- Annual Revenue: $8.4 billion
- R&D 2002: $1.15 billion
- Sales Force Size: 2,200
- Number of employees: 33,000 worldwide
- Operating in countries worldwide: 100
- Ranks in the top 20 for world-wide pharmaceutical companies.
- Expects to acquire Lorex Pharmaceuticals in 2002.
- They are well established in Europe and have a considerable presence in Japan.
- Sanofi is the second largest pharmaceutical company in France.
- Sanofi has 23 products in Phase II and Phase III trials with 52 compounds in development.
- Their sales and marketing department is staffed by 11,015 people.
- They had strong growth in the first half of 2003.
- Sanofi-Synthelabo has 6,718 people in R&D.

Major Products & Therapeutic Areas

Cardiovascular	Neuroscience	Oncology	Anti-Inflammatory
Avapro: hypertension	Ambien: insomnia	Eloxatine: colorectal cancer	Hyalgan: osteoarthritis pain
Primacor: AHF	Stilnox; Depakine		
Cordarone: arrhythmia	Dogmatil; Solian	Eligard: advanced prostate cancer	
Ticlid: platelet aggregation	Aspegic		
Plavix: MI; stroke			
Avalide: hypertension			

Cardiovascular	Women's Health	Specialty	Other
Aprovel	Prenate Advance: vitamin for pregnant and postnatal women	Xatral: Benign Prostatic Hypertrophy	Arixtra: blood clots following orthopedic surgery
Fraxiparine			
Tildiem		Elitek: plasma uric acid in cancer patients	Avapro: diabetic neuropathy
Corotrope			
Kerlone			

Pipeline Products

Neuroscience	Oncology	Internal Medicine	Cardiovascular/ Thrombosis
Befloxatone: depression	Oxaliplatin: advanced colorectal cancer	Xatral: BPH	Pentasaccharide: blood clots
Xaliproden: ALS	Tirapazamine	Fasturtec: acute hyperuricemia	dronedarone

173

Schering-Plough Corporation

2000 Galloping Hill Road
Kenilworth, NJ 07033-0530
Phone: 908-289-4000
Web: schering-plough.com

Highlights

- Chairman/CEO: Fred Hassan
- Annual Revenue: $10.2 billion
- R&D 2002: $1.4 billion
- Sales Force Size: 2500
- Number of employees: 29,800 worldwide
- Operating in countries worldwide: 125
- They market Claritin, the #1 selling antihistamine in the world.
- Rated one of the 100 "best managed" companies by *Industry Week* Magazine.
- Recognized leader in biotechnology, genomics and gene therapy fields.
- Schering markets their products in the U.S. under the Schering Laboratories and Key Pharmaceuticals labels.
- They market generics through their Warrick Pharmaceuticals unit.
- Collaborating with Merck to develop and co-market Zetia.
- October 23, 2000 announced collaboration effort with ALK-Abello on tablet-based immunotherapy for grass pollen allergy symptoms.

Major Products & Therapeutic Areas

Allergy/ Respiratory	Anti-Infective/ Oncology	Anti-Infective/ Oncology	Dermatology
Clarinex	Intron A/PEG-Intron	Rebetol	Diprosone
Caritin/Claritin D	Ethyol	Temodar	Diprolene
Vancenase AQ	Eulexin	Caelyn: breast cancer	Diprolene AF
Vanceril DS	Fareston		Elocon
Nasonex AQ	Leucomax		Lotrisone
Proventil/HFA; Uni-Dur	Rebetron		
Foradil			

Cardiovascular	Cardiovascular	Anti-Inflammatory	Other
Imdur; Integrilin	Nitro-Dur	Remicade: ankylosing spondylitis	
K-Dur	Zetia: cholesterol		

Pipeline Products

Allergy/Respiratory	Anti-Infective/ Oncology	Inflammation/ Metabolic	Cardiovascular/ Neuroscience
Asmanex: asthma	Fareston, Temozolomide and Toremefine: cancer	Interleukin-10	Integrelin: AMI
Claritin EZ: fast-dissolving antihistamine	Interleukin-4: GI cancer	Prometrium: hormonal imbalance	Taloza: epilepsy
Clarinex D: 24 hr.	Leucomax: low WBC	Remicade: early RA	
Claritin/Singulair	Sarasar: lung cancer	Zetia/ZoCor: lipid lowering	

Wyeth Pharmaceuticals

Wyeth Collegeville
500 Areola Road
Collegeville, PA 19426
Phone: 610-902-1200
Web: wyeth.com

Highlights

- Chairman/CEO: Robert Essner
- Annual Revenue: $14.1 billion
- R&D 2002: $2.1 billion
- Sales Force Size: 4300
- Number of employees: 44,000 worldwide
- Operating in countries worldwide: 140
- Wyeth was started by John and Frank Wyeth in 1860.
- AHP changed it's name to Wyeth Mar. 2002.
- Leader in protein therapeutics research.

- Has more than 70 pipeline products.
- Compounded bank contains more than 500,000 unique chemical entities.
- Wyeth has 37 manufacturing facilities in 17 locations around the globe.
- Created the Women's Health Research Institute in 1993.
- Collaborated with *Genetics Institute* for therapeutic protein discovery in 1998.
- AHP sold 41% of its Immunex shares to Amgen, Inc. for cash and 8% Amgen stock.

Major Products & Therapeutic Areas

Cardiovascular/ Neuroscience	Infectious Disease	Musculoskeletal/ Oncology	Transplant/ Neuroscience
Altace: hypertension & reduction of stroke and MI	Suprax: middle ear infection	Embrel: severe rheumatoid arthritis	Rapamune: organ rejection
Cordarone I.V.: arrhythmias	Zosyn/Tazocin: moderate to severe infections	Synvisc: injectable device for osteoarthritis- knee	Effexor/XR: depression/ anxiety
Sonata: insomnia		Mylotarg: cancer/AML	Sonata: insomnia/ epilepsy
Phenergan: nausea		Neumega: chemo patients	

Vaccines	Women's Health	Gastrointestinal	Hemophilia
FluShield; FluMist	Alesse: oral contraceptive	Protonix: erosive esophagitis	BeneFIX: Hemophilia B
Influenza Virus Vaccine	Premarin/Prempro/ Premphase: menopausal symtoms and osteoporosis	Phenergan: nausea & vomiting	ReFacto: Hemophilia A
Trivalent, Types A & B			
Pnu-Immune 23/ Prevnar: pneumococcal	Conpremin		
Hib Titer H-b	Loette		

Pipeline Products

Neuroscience/ Transplant	Infectious Disease/ Hemophilia	Musculoskeletal/ Oncology	Women's Health/ Vaccines
Sonata IV	Zosyn: extended indications	Enbrel: psoriasis	Premarin/Bazedoxifene: osteoporosis/vasomotor symptoms
Rapamune: kidney transplant	Tigecycline: serious polymicrobic infections	RhBMP-2: bone fractures	
Effexor XR: panic disorder	ReFacto: F VIII-alb free	CCI-779: breast cancer	Prempro: menopause

Appendix B
Pharmaceutical Companies

PHARMACEUTICAL COMPANY	**WEB SITE ADDRESS**
3 M Pharmaceuticals	http://www.3m.com/
Abbott Laboratories	http://www.abbott.com/
Abgenix, Inc.	http://www.abgenix.com/
Access Pharmaceuticals, Inc.	http://www.accesspharmac.com
Active Pass Pharmaceuticals	http://www.activepass.com
Agouron Pharmaceuticals, Inc.	http://www.agouron.com/
AidsRX	http://aidsdrugs.com/
Akorn Ophthalmics, USA	http://www.akorn.com/
Alcon	http://www.alconlabs.com/
Alexion Pharmaceuticals	http://www.alexionpharm.com/
Allergan	http://www.allergan.com/
Alliance Pharmaceutical Corp.	http://www.allp.com/
Almirall, Europe	http://www.intercom.es/almirall/
Alpharma	http://www.alpharma.com/
AltiMed Pharmaceutical Company	http://www.altimed.com/
ALZA Corp.	http://www.alza.com/
American Home Products Corporation	http://www.ahp.com/
AMGEN	http://www.amgen.com/
AMRAD	http://www.amrad.com.au/
Amstelfarma	http://www.amstelfarma.nl/
Amylin	http://www.amylin.com/

Apex Laboratories Ltd., India	http://www.apexlabs.com/
Apothecus	http://www.apothecus.com/
APS/Berk, UK	http://www.aps-berk.com/
Ares-Serono International	http://www.serono.com/
ARIAD Pharmaceuticals, Inc.	http://www.ariad.com/
Aronex Pharmaceuticals, Inc	http://www.aronex.com/
ArQule	http://www.arqule.com/into.html
Arris Pharmaceutical	http://www.arris.com/
ASAC Pharmaceutical International	http://asac.net/
ASTA Medica Ltd	http://www.astamedica.com/
AstraZeneca Group	http://www.astrazeneca.com/
Atlantic Pharmaceuticals, Inc.	http://www.atlan.com/
Atrix Laboratories, Inc.	http://www.atrixlabs.com/
Avant Immunotherapeutics	http://www.avantimmune.com
Aventis	http://www2.aventis.com/
Aviron	http://www.aviron.com/
Azupharma GmbH	http://www.azupharma.de/
Barr Laboratories, Inc. - USA	http://www.barrlabs.com/
BASF	http://www.basf.com/
Bausch & Lomb	http://www.bausch.com/
Bayer	http://www.bayer.com/
Baxter International Inc.	http://www.baxter.com/
Becton Dickinson	http://www.bd.com/
Beiersdorf-Lilly	http://www.beiersdorf-lilly.de
Belmed	http://www.I-connect.ru/~belmed/
Berlex Laboratories, Inc.	http://www.berlex.com/
Bertek Pharmaceuticals Inc.	http://www.bertek.com/
Beximco	http://www.beximcorp.com/
Bilim Pharmaceutical Inc.	http://www.bilimpharma.com/
Biochem Pharma	http://www.biochempharma.com/
Biogen, Inc.	http://www.biogen.com
Bioglan	http://www.bioglan.com
Biomes	http://www.biomes.com
Biorex	http://www.biorex.hu/
Biotech Holdings, Inc.	http://www.biotechltd.com/
Boehringer Ingelheim	http://www.boehringer-ingelheim.com/
Boot	http://www.boots.co.uk
Braun Melsungen	http://bbraun.com
Bristol-Myers Squibb	http://www.bms.com/
Britannia Pharmaceuticals Limited	http://www.britannia-pharm.co.uk/
Cadus Pharmaceutical Corporation	http://www.cadus.com/
Caleb Pharmaceuticals, Inc.	http://www.caleb-pharm.com/
Cantab Pharmaceuticals	http://www.cantab.co.uk/
CCL Pharmaceuticals, Pakistan	http://www.cclpharma.com/
Celltech, Plc	http://www.celltech.co.uk/

Central Pharmaceutical Co., Ltd., China	http://www.ipine.com/
Cephalon, Inc.	http://www.cephalon.com/
Chiron	http://www.chiron.com/
Chiroscience	http://www.chiroscience.com/
Chugai Pharmaceutical Co. Ltd.	http://www.chugai.co.uk/
Ciba (Novartis)	http://www.ciba.com/
CollaGenex Pharmaceuticals, Inc.	http://www.collagenex.com/
ConvaTec	http://www.convatec.com/
Cortecs plc	http://www.cortecs.com/
Coulter Pharmaceutical	http://www.coulterpharm.com
Covance, Inc.	http://www.covance.com/
Cubist Pharmaceuticals, Inc.	http://www.cubist.com/
Curis Pharmaceuticals	http://www.curis.com/
CP Pharmaceuticals	http://cppharma.co.uk/
Dimethaid Research Inc. - Canada	http://www.dimethaid.com/
Douglas Pharmaceuticals	http://www.douglas.co.nz/index.cfm
Dow Hickam Pharmaceuticals, USA	http://www.dowhickam.com/
Draxis Health, Inc.	http://www.draxis.com/
Dura Pharmaceuticals, USA	http://www.durapharm.com/
Dupont Pharmaceuticals Company	http://www.dupontpharma.com/
Duramed Pharmaceuticals, Inc.	http://www.duramed.com/
EBEWE Arzneimittel GmBH	http://www.ebewe.com.at/
Efroze Chemical Industries Ltd., Pakistan	http://www.efroze.com/
Eisai Inc., USA	http://www.eisai.com/
Elan Corporation, plc	http://www.elancorp.com/
Eli Lilly and Company	http://www.lilly.com/
Endo Pharmaceuticals Inc., USA	http://www.endo.com/
EntreMed	http://www.entremed.com/
Enzon, Inc.	http://www.enzon.com/
Epimmune	http://www.epimmune.com/
Esteve Group, International	http://www.esteve.com/
Ethicon, Inc.	http://www.ethiconinc.com/
F H Faulding & Co Limited	http://www.faulding.com.au/
Ferring Pharmaceuticals	http://www.ferring.com/
Fielding Pharmaceutical Company	http://www.fieldingcompany.com/
Fischer Pharmaceutical Laboratories	http://www.dr-fischer.com/
Flemington Pharmaceutical Corporation	http://www.flemington-pharma.com/
Forest Laboratories	http://www.frx.com/
Fougera	http://www.fougera.com/
Fujisawa Pharmaceutical Co., Ltd.	http://www.fujisawa.co.jp/
Gate Pharmaceuticals, USA	http://www.gatepharma.com/
GelTex Pharmaceuticals	http://www.geltex.com/
Genentech, Inc.	http://www.gene.com/
Genetics Institute, Inc.	http://www.genetics.com/
Genzyme Corporation	http://www.genzyme.com/pharm/

Gilead Sciences	http://www.gilead.com/
Glaxo Wellcome	http://www.glaxowellcome.co.uk/
Glenwood	http://www.glenwood-llc.com/
Groupement Provincial ... Médicament	http://www.gpim.org/
Guilford Pharmaceuticals, Inc.	http://www.guilfordpharm.com/
Gynetics, Inc.	http://www.gynetics.com/
Heel	http://www.heel.de/
Helios Pharmaceuticals	http://www.helios-pharm/
Hemosol, Inc.	http://www.hemosol.com/
Hermal	http://www.hermal.de/
Heumann Pharma	http://www.heumann.de/
Hexal	http://www.hexal.de
H. Lundbeck	http://www.lundbeck.com/
Hoechst	http://www.hoechst.com
Hoechst Marion Roussel (Now Adventis)	http://www.hmri.com
Hoffmann-La Roche, Inc.	http://www.roche.com/
Hovid Sdn Bhd	http://www.hovid.com/
Human Genome Sciences	http://www.hgsi.com/
IBSA	http://www.ibsa.ch/
ICI	http://www.ici.com/
ICI India Pharmaceuticals, India	http://www.icipharms.com/
ICN Pharmaceuticals, Inc.	http://www.icnpharm.com/
ID Biomedical Corporation	http://www.idbiomed.com/
IDEC Pharmaceuticals Corporation	http://www.idecpharm.com/
Ilsanta, Europe	http://www.ilsanta.lt/
Immunex Corporation	http://www.immunex.com/
Incyte Pharmaceuticals	http://www.incyte.com/
Interferon Sciences, Inc.	http://www.interferonsciences.com/
InterMune Pharmaceuticals	http://www.intermune.com/
Ipsen Limited, UK	http://www.ipsen.ltd.uk/
Isis Pharmaceuticals	http://www.isisph.com/
Janssen-Cilag NV	http://www.janssen-cilag.com/
Janseen Pharmaceutica, Inc.	http://www.janseen.com/
Jenapharm	http://www.jenapharm.de/
Johnson & Johnson	http://www.jnj.com/
Jones Pharm Inc., USA	http://www.jmedpharma.com/
Key Oncologics	http://www.icon.com.za/
King Pharmaceuticals	http://www.kingpharm.com/
Knoll - International	http://www.knoll.de/
Knoll Pharmaceutical Company	http://www.knoll-pharma.com/
Kos Pharmaceuticals, Inc.	http://www.kospharm.com/
Kramer Laboratories	http://www.kramerlabs.com/
KV Pharmaceuticals	http://www.kvpharma.com/
Laboratorios Rubio, S.A.	http://www.laboratoriosrubio.com/
Lacer, S.A.	http://www.lacer.es/

LaJolla Pharmaceuticals	http://www.ljpc.com/
Lee Pharmaceuticals	http://www.leepharmaceuticals.com/
Leo Pharmaceutical Products Ltd.	http://www.leo-pharma.com/
Lichtwer Pharma	http://www.lichtwer.de/
Ligand Pharmaceuticals, Inc.	http://www.ligand.com/
LigoCyte Pharmaceuticals, Inc.	http://www.ligocyte.com/
Liposome Company, Inc.	http://www.lipo.com/
LTS Lohmann	http://www.ltslohmann.de/
Mallinckrodt	http://www.mallinckrodt.com
Matrix Pharmaceuticals, Inc.	http://www.matx.com/
Maxim Pharmaceuticals	http://www.maxim.com/
Medeva PLC	http://www.medeva.co.uk/
Medicis Pharmaceutical Corp.	http://www.medicis.com/
Menarini, S.A	http://www.menarini.es/
Merck & Co., Inc.	http://www.merck.com/
Merck KGaA	http://www.merck.de/english/index.htm
Merz + Co.	http://www.merz.de/
MGI Pharma Inc.	http://www.mgipharma.com/
Microcide Pharmaceuticals	http://www.microcide.com/
Minority Pharma	http://asapcons.com/minority
Mission Pharmacal Company	http://www.missionpharmacal.com
ML Laboratories	http://www.mllabs.co.uk/
Mochida Pharmaceutical Co., Ltd.	http://www.mochida.co.jp/
Monarch Pharmaceuticals	http://www.monarchpharm.com/
Monsanto (Searle Pharmaceuticals)	http://www.monsanto.com/
Mylan Laboratories, Inc., USA	http://www.mylan.com/
NeoTherapeutics, Inc.	http://www.neotherapeutics.com/
Neurogen	http://www.neurogen.com/
Nexell Therapeutics, Inc.	http://www.nexellinc.com/
NeXstart	http://www.nexstar.com/
Nortran Pharmaceuticals, Inc.	http://www.nortran.com/
Novartis (formerly Sandoz)	http://www.novartis.com/
Novartis Pharmaceuticals Worldwide	http://www.novartis-us-pharma.com/
Novogen	http://www.novogen.com/
Novo Nordisk	http://www.novo.dk/index.asp
Novopharm Ltd.	http://www.novopharmusa.com/
NPS Pharmaceuticals, Inc.	http://www.npsp.com/
Nutromax Laboratories	http://www.nutramaxlabs.com/
Nycomed Amersham plc	http://www.amersham.co.uk/
Onyx Pharmaceuticals	http://www.onyx-pharm.com/
Orchid Chemicals & Pharmaceuticals Ltd.	http://www.orchidpharma.com/
Organon	http://www.organon.com/
Orion Pharma	http://www.orion.fi/
Ortho-McNeil Pharmaceuticals	http://www.ortho-mcneil.com/
OSI Pharmaceuticals, Inc.	http://www.osip.com/

Otsuka America Pharmaceuticals, Inc.	http://www.otsuka.comjp/cop-e.htm
Oxford GlycoSciences	http://www.ogs.com/
PanDrugs	http://www.pandrug.com
Paracelsian, Inc.	http://www.paracelsian.com/
Parke-Davis	http://www.parke-davis.com/
Pascoe	http://www.pascoe.de/
PathoGenesis Corp.	http://www.pathogenesis.com/
Penwest Pharmaceuticals Co.	http://www.penw.com/
Peptech Limited	http://www.peptech.com/
Perrigo	http://www.perrigo.com/
Pfizer	http://www.pfizer.com/
Pharbita	http://www.pharbita-pb.de/
Pharmacia	http://www.pharmacia.se/
Pharmacia & Upjohn	http://www.pnu.com/
Pharmacyclics	http://www.pcyc.com/
Pharmanetics	http://www.pharmanetics.com/
Proctor & Gamble Company	http://www.pg.com/
Procyon Biopharma, Inc.	http://www.procyonbiopharma.com/
Procyte	http://www.procyte.com/
Progenics Pharmaceuticals, Inc.	http://www.progenics.com
Provalis	http://www.cortecs.com/
PT Anugraph Argon Medica	http://www.anugraph-argon.com
PT Darya-Varia Laboratoria	http://www.darya-varia.com/
Purdue Pharma L.P.	http://www.pharma.com/
QLT Phototherapeutics	http://www.nserc.ca/sen/
Questcor Pharmaceuticals, Inc.	http://www.questcor.com/
Quintiles Transnational Corp.	http://www.quintiles.com/
R & J Engineering Corp.	http://www.rjengineering.com/
Ranbaxy Laboratories Ltd.	http://www.ranbaxy.com/
Ratiopharm	http://www.ratiopharm.de/
Regeneron Pharmaceuticals, Inc.	http://www.regeneron.com/
Remington Pharmaceuticals. LTD-Pakistan	http://www.remingtonco.com/
RepliGen Corporation	http://www.repligen.com/
Rhone-Poulenc	http://www.rhone-poulenc.com/
Rhone-Poulenc Rorer, Inc.	http://www.rp-rorer.com/
Ribozyme Pharmaceuticals, Inc.	http://www.rpi.com/
Roche Canada	http://www.rochecanada.com/
Roche Group	http://www.roche.com/
Roxane Laboratories, Inc.	http://www.roxane.com/Roxane/
Sagitta	http://www.sagitta.de/
SangStat	http://www.sangstat.com/default.htm
Sanofi-Synthelabo, Inc.	http://www.sanofi-synthelaboUS.com
Sanorania	http://www.sanorania.de/
Sai Pharmaceutical Works, Asia	http://www.saipharma.com/
Salix Pharmaceuticals	http://www.salixltd.com/

Sankyo Co., Ltd.	http://www.sankyo.co.jp/
Sanochemia Group	http://www.sanochemia.at/
Schein Pharmaceutical	http://www.schein-rx.com/
Schering-Plough Corporation	http://www.schering-ploush.com/
Schering	http://www.schering.de/
Schwarz Pharma	http://www.schwarz-pharma.de/
Scios, Inc.	http://www.sciosinc.com/
Searle	http://www.searlehealthnet.com/
SEQUUS Pharmaceuticals	http://www.sequus.com/alza_splash.html
Sheffield Pharmaceuticals	http://www.sheffieldpharm.com/
Shire Pharmaceuticals Group, plc	http://www.shire.com/
SIGA Pharmaceuticals, Inc.	http://www.siga.com/
Sigma Tau Pharmaceuticals, USA	http://www.sigmatau.com/
SmithKline Beecham	http://www.sb.com/
Solka Laboratories Inc., Central America	http://www.ibw.com
Solvay	http://www.solvay.com/
Sonus Pharmaceuticals	http://www.sonuspharma.com/
SP Pharmaceuticals	http://www.sppharma.com
Stada	http://www.stada.de/
Steigerwald	http://www.steigerwald.de/
Strathmann	http://www.strathmann.de/
StressGen Biotechnologies Corp.	http://www2.stressgen.com/stressgen/
SuperGen	http://www.supergen.com/
Synsorb	http://www.synsorb.com/
Synthelabo	http://www.synthelabo.fr/
Synthon BV	http://www.synthon.nl/
Takeda Pharma GmbH	http://www.takeda.de/
Takeda Pharmaceuticals America, Inc., USA	http://www.takedapharm.com/
Tanade Seiyaku Co., Inc.	http://www.tanabe.com.jp/
TAP Pharmaceuticals	http://www.tap.com/
Taro Pharmaceuticals	http://www.taropharma.com/
Technilab Pharma Inc.	http://www.technilab.ca/
Telluride Pharmaceutical Corporation	http://www.tellpharm.com/
Texas Biotechnology Corp., USA	http://www.tbc.com/
Togal-Werk	http://www.togal.de/
Trega Biosciences, Inc.	http://www.trega.com/
Trimeris	http://www.trimeris.com/
Triangle Pharmaceuticals, Inc.	http://www.tripharm.com/
UCB	http://www.ucb.be/
United -Guardian, Inc.	http://www.u-g.com/
United Therapeutics	http://www.unither.com/
U.S. Bioscience	http://www.usbio.com/
Vectorpharma	http://www.vectorpharma.com/
Vertex Pharmaceuticals, Inc.	http://www.vpharm.com/
Vainex S.A., Greece	http://www.vianex.gr/

Vindas Chemical Industries Ltd.	http://www.vindas.com/
Vital Drugs & Pharmaceuticals	http://www.angelfire.com/
Warner-Lambert	http://www.warner-lambert.com/
Wuelfing Pharma	http://www.wuelfing.de/
Yamanouchi, USA, Inc.	http://www.yamanouchi.com/
Zambon	http://www.zambon.it/
Zeneca	http://www.zeneca.com/
Zila, Inc.	http://www.zila.com/

More Books by Best-Selling Author Jane Williams

Professional Pharmaceutical Selling
2004
ISBN: 0-9704153-7-0

Professional Pharmaceutical Selling, scheduled for release in the first quarter of 2005, contains more specific pharmaceutical selling information for the prospective pharmaceutical sales professional and the current pharmaceutical sales representative. This book contains information critical to achieving stellar sales success within the pharmaceutical industry and includes essential information on managed care selling.

Sell Yourself! Master the Job Interview Process
2004
ISBN: 0-9704153-8-9

Sell Yourself is scheduled for release in December of 2004 and contains vital, specific information detailing how to interview successfully. All of the research and industry knowledge in the world will not guarantee anyone a job. The position always goes to the person who excels at self-selling. Jane Williams, a master at selling and author of the best-selling pharmaceutical sales career guide, the *Insider's Guide to the World of Pharmaceutical Sales* explains self-selling techniques that will help anyone successfully interview for any career field.

Look for these titles at local and on-line bookstores.

Publisher Contact Information:

Principle Publications
4101 W. Green Oaks Blvd.
Suite 305-585
Arlington, TX 76016
http://www.principlepublications.com